LEABHARLANNA P...

...uble Helix

JAMES D. WATSON

Level 6

Retold by David Maule
Scientific Consultant: Dr Peter Jeppesen,
MRC Human Genetics Unit, Edinburgh
Series Editors: Andy Hopkins and Jocelyn Potter

Pearson Education Limited
Edinburgh Gate, Harlow,
Essex CM20 2JE, England
and Associated Companies throughout the world.

ISBN 0 582 451817

First published in Great Britain by Weidenfeld & Nicolson,
part of the Orion Publishing Group, 1968
This edition first published by Penguin 2001

Original copyright © James D. Watson 1968
Text copyright © Penguin Books 2001
Illustrations by Nick Hawken
The moral rights of the author have been asserted

Typeset by Pantek Arts Ltd, Maidstone, Kent
Set in 11/14pt Bembo
Printed in Spain by Mateu Cromo, S.A. Pinto (Madrid)

Published by Pearson Education Limited in association with
Penguin Books Ltd, both companies being subsidiaries of Pearson Plc

For a complete list of the titles available in the Penguin Readers series please write to your local
Pearson Education office or to: Marketing Department, Penguin Longman Publishing,
80 Strand, London, WC2R 0RL.

Contents

Introduction

In the autumn of 1951, I came to the Cavendish Laboratory of Cambridge University to join a small group of physicists and chemists working on the structure of proteins ...

James Watson is a biologist from Chicago. He comes to Cambridge to learn X-ray crystallography because he feels it is the way to discover the structure of DNA. He is twenty-three years old. Francis Crick is older – but much noisier. He talks non-stop in a loud voice and has an even louder laugh. Not many people can work with Crick; some, including his boss, Sir Lawrence Bragg, find it hard to be in the same room. But with Crick, Watson finds a meeting of minds. Together they set off on the road that will lead, after many wrong turnings, to the double helix.

Others travel with them on the way: Maurice Wilkins, from the King's College laboratory in London, and his colleague Rosalind Franklin, both of whom produce X-ray diffraction photographs that are essential to the work. And Linus Pauling, America's finest chemist, who is moving in the same direction – and doing his best to get there first.

In 1962, Watson, Crick and Wilkins each received the Nobel Prize for their work with DNA. By this time Rosalind Franklin was dead, killed by cancer four years earlier at the age of thirty-seven. Many people have said that Watson's description of Franklin in this book is unfair, and Watson later accepted that this was true. Also, in the years before her death, both Watson and Francis Crick got to know Rosalind Franklin better, and saw her as the hard-working and successful scientist that she was.

But this is James Watson's description of an earlier time. It is a younger man's story and it tells of the way that human thought moves forward – of how scientific progress is made.

Chapter 1 The Cavendish Laboratory

I have never seen Francis Crick in a modest mood. This has nothing to do with his present fame. Already he is much talked about, usually with great respect, and one day he may be considered an equal to Rutherford or Bohr.* But this was not true when, in the autumn of 1951, I came to the Cavendish Laboratory of Cambridge University to join a small group of physicists and chemists working on the structure of proteins. At that time Francis was thirty-five, but almost totally unknown. Although some of his colleagues respected his quick mind and frequently asked his advice, he was often not appreciated, and most people thought he talked too much.

Leading the unit to which Francis belonged was Max Perutz, an Austrian-born chemist who came to England in 1936. He had been collecting X-ray diffraction data from protein crystals for over ten years and was just beginning to get results. Helping him was Sir Lawrence Bragg, the director of the Cavendish. For forty years Bragg, a Nobel Prize winner and one of the first crystallographers, had been watching X-ray diffraction methods solve structures of increasing difficulty. In the immediate post-war years he was especially keen on the possibility of solving the structure of proteins, the most complex of all molecules.

Somewhere between Bragg the theorist and Perutz the experimenter was Francis, who occasionally did experiments but was more often interested in theories for solving protein structures. Often he had a new idea, became enormously excited,

*Ernest Rutherford (1871–1937) and, later, Niels Bohr (1885–1962) introduced the concepts from which modern atomic theory has developed. Bohr also worked on the atomic bomb.

1

and would immediately tell anyone who was willing to listen. A day or two later he would often realize that his theory did not work and return to experiments, until he got bored with them and turned again to theory.

These ideas brought an atmosphere of excitement to the laboratory, where experiments usually lasted several months to years. This came partly from the volume of Crick's voice; he talked louder and faster than anyone else, and when he laughed everyone knew where he was in the Cavendish. Most people enjoyed these exciting moments, especially when we had time to listen closely and to tell him when we lost the logic of his argument. But there was one significant exception. Conversations with Crick frequently upset Sir Lawrence Bragg, and the sound of his voice was often enough to make Bragg move to a safer room. Only infrequently would he come to tea in the Cavendish, since it meant he had to hear Crick's loud voice in the tea room. Even if he stayed away, Bragg was not completely safe. On two occasions the corridor outside his office was flooded with water pouring out of a laboratory in which Crick was working. Francis, with his interest in theory, had not properly connected the rubber tubes to his pump.

At the time of my arrival, Francis's theories spread far beyond the boundaries of protein crystallography. Anything important would attract him, and he frequently visited other laboratories to see which new experiments had been done. Though he was generally polite to colleagues who did not realize the real meaning of their latest experiments, he did not attempt to hide this fact from them. Almost immediately, he would suggest a number of new experiments that would confirm his analysis. Moreover, he could not stop himself from later telling anybody who would listen how his clever new idea might move science forward.

As a result, an unspoken but real fear of Crick existed, especially among his more junior colleagues. The quick manner in which he seized their facts and tried to make sense of them frequently made his friends worry that he would actually succeed. This would show the world the loose thinking that was hidden behind the good manners and polite conversation of the Cambridge colleges.

Though he had the right to dine one night a week at Caius College, Francis did not belong to the staff of any college. Partly this was his own choice. Clearly he did not want the unnecessary responsibility of teaching students. Another problem was his laugh, against which many academics would certainly rebel if they had to hear it more than once a week. I am sure this occasionally bothered Francis, although he knew that most college dinners were dominated by boring, middle-aged men incapable of either amusing or educating him. His friends, who knew he was an entertaining dinner companion, made much effort on his behalf, but they were never able to hide the fact that Francis might get into an argument with anyone present at the table.

◆

Before my arrival in Cambridge, Francis only occasionally thought about deoxyribonucleic acid (DNA) and its role in genetics. This was not because he thought it was uninteresting. Quite the opposite. A major reason why he had left physics and developed an interest in biology had been the reading in 1946 of *What is Life?* by the respected theoretical physicist Erwin Schrödinger. This book stated the belief that genes were the most important parts of living cells and that, to understand what life is, we must know how genes act. When Schrödinger wrote his book (1944) there was a general acceptance that genes were special types of protein molecules. But almost at the same time the bacteriologist O. T. Avery was carrying out experiments in New York which showed that physical characteristics could be passed from one bacterial cell to another by purified DNA molecules.

Since DNA was known to occur in the chromosomes of all cells, Avery's experiments strongly suggested that future experiments would show that all genes were made up of DNA. If true, this meant to Francis that DNA, not proteins, would provide the key to enable us to find out how the genes determined, among other characteristics, the colour of our hair and eyes, probably our intelligence and maybe even our ability to amuse others.

Of course, there were scientists who thought that the evidence favouring DNA was unclear and preferred to believe that genes were protein molecules. Francis did not worry about them. One could not be a successful scientist without realizing that, in contrast to the popular belief supported by newspapers and the mothers of scientists, a large number of scientists are not only narrow-minded and dull, but also just stupid.

Francis, however, was not then prepared to jump into the DNA world. Its basic importance did not seem a strong enough reason to lead him out of the protein field which he had worked in for only two years and was just beginning to understand thoroughly. In addition, his colleagues at the Cavendish were only slightly interested in the nucleic acids, and even in the best of financial circumstances, it would take two or three years to set up a new study group which would use X-rays to look at the DNA structure.

Moreover, such a decision would create an awkward personal situation. At this time molecular work on DNA in England was considered to be the personal property of Maurice Wilkins, who worked at King's College, London.* Like Francis, Maurice had been a physicist and also used X-ray diffraction as his principal method of study. It would have looked very bad if Francis had

---

*King's College, London: a part of the University of London – not to be confused with King's College, Cambridge.

4

jumped in on a problem that Maurice had worked on for several years. The matter was even worse because the two, almost equal in age, knew each other quite well. Maurice was unmarried, and before Francis remarried they had frequently met for lunch or dinner to talk about science.

It would have been much easier if they had been living in different countries. In England, all the important people, if not related by marriage, seemed to know each other, and it would have been seen as unfair for Francis to move in on Maurice's problem. In France, where this sense of unfairness did not exist, these problems would not have occurred. The States would also not have permitted such a situation to develop. One would not expect someone at Berkeley* to ignore a challenging problem just because someone at Cal Tech† had started first. In England, however, it simply would not look right.

Even worse, Maurice continually annoyed Francis by never seeming enthusiastic enough about DNA. Moreover, it was increasingly difficult to take Maurice's mind off his assistant, Rosalind Franklin. He was not in love with Rosy, as we called her from a distance. Just the opposite – almost from the moment she arrived in Maurice's laboratory, they began to upset each other. Maurice, a beginner in X-ray diffraction work, wanted some professional help and hoped that Rosy, a trained crystallographer, could speed up his work. Rosy, however, did not see the situation this way. She claimed that she had been given DNA as her own problem and she refused to think of herself as Maurice's assistant.

I suspect that in the beginning Maurice hoped that Rosy would calm down. But she was a determined woman. By choice, she did not emphasize her female qualities. Though her features

*Berkeley: part of the University of California.
† Cal Tech: a technology college in California.

5

were strong, she might have been quite attractive if she had taken even a mild interest in clothes. She did not. There was never any lipstick to contrast with her straight black hair, while her dresses showed no imagination at all. So it would have been easy to believe that she was the product of a dissatisfied mother who emphasized the importance of a professional career as an alternative to marriage to a dull man. But this was not the case. In fact, she was the daughter of a comfortable and cultured banking family.

Clearly Rosy had to go or be controlled. The former was obviously preferable because her aggressive moods made it very difficult for Maurice to think in peace about DNA. There were times when he could see some reason for her complaints. For example, King's had two social rooms, one for men, the other for women, certainly an arrangement from the past. But he was not responsible, and it was no pleasure to be blamed for the fact that the women's social room was small and dirty while money had been spent to make him and his friends more comfortable when they had their morning coffee.

Unfortunately, Maurice could not see any decent way to sack Rosy. First, she had been given the impression that she had a job for several years. Also, she had a good brain. If she could keep her emotions under control, there would be a good chance she could really help him. But hoping and waiting for relations to improve was taking a chance, since Cal Tech's great chemist Linus Pauling was not limited by the rules of British fair play. Sooner or later Linus, who was just fifty, was bound to try for the most important of all scientific prizes. We knew that Pauling could not be the greatest of all chemists without realizing that DNA was the most golden of all molecules. Moreover, there was definite proof. Maurice had received a letter from Linus asking for a copy of the crystalline DNA X-ray photographs. After some hesitation he wrote back saying he wanted to look more closely at the data before releasing the pictures.

Chapter 2 The Alpha Helix

It was Wilkins who had first excited me about X-ray work on DNA. This happened in Naples when a small scientific meeting was held on the structures of the large molecules found in living cells. Then it was the spring of 1951, before I knew of Francis Crick's existence. Already I was much involved with DNA, since I had been sent to Europe to learn its biochemistry. My interest in DNA had grown out of a desire, which started while I was a senior in college, to learn what the gene was. Later, in graduate school at Indiana University, it was my hope that the gene might be solved without me learning any chemistry. This was partly due to laziness as a student at the University of Chicago, where I had managed to avoid taking any chemistry or physics courses which looked of even medium difficulty. Briefly, I was encouraged to learn chemistry at Indiana, but after I used a bare flame to warm up some petrol, I was excused from doing any more. It was safer to allow an uneducated Ph.D than to risk another explosion.

So I managed to avoid learning any chemistry until I went to Copenhagen to work with the biochemist Herman Kalckar. Travelling abroad at first seemed the perfect solution to the complete lack of chemical facts in my head, a condition at times encouraged by my main teacher at Indiana, the Italian-trained bacteriologist Salvador Luria. He hated most chemists, especially those who did commercial work. Kalckar, however, was obviously a civilized man, and Luria hoped that, while working with him, I would learn something about the subject.

Then Luria's experiments mainly dealt with the multiplication of bacterial viruses. For some years the suspicion had existed among the more original thinkers in genetics that viruses were a type of basic gene. If so, the best way to find out what a gene was and how it copied itself was to study viruses. So because the simplest viruses were the bacterial ones, a growing number of scientists, between 1940 and 1950, began to study them. Leading this group were Luria and his German-born friend, the theoretical physicist Max Delbrück, who was then in a senior position at Cal Tech. While Delbrück kept hoping that purely genetic tricks could solve the problem, Luria more often wondered whether the real answer would come only after the chemical structure of a virus (gene) had been cracked open. Deep down he knew that it is impossible to describe the behaviour of something when you do not know what it is. So, knowing he could never make himself learn chemistry, Luria felt the best thing would be to send me, his first serious student, to a chemist.

He had no difficulty deciding between a protein chemist and a nucleic-acid chemist. Though only about one half the mass of a bacterial virus was DNA (the other half being protein), Avery's experiment made it seem like the essential genetic material. So working out DNA's chemical structure might be the essential chemical step in learning how genes copied themselves. However, in contrast to the proteins, the solid chemical facts known about DNA were very few. Only a few chemists worked with it and, except for the fact that nucleic acids were very large molecules built up from smaller building blocks (the nucleotides), there was almost nothing chemical that the geneticist could begin to work with. Moreover, the chemists who did work on DNA were almost always organic chemists with no interest in genetics. Kalckar was a bright exception. In the summer of 1945 he had come to the laboratory at Cold Spring Harbor, New York, to take Delbrück's course on bacterial viruses. So both Luria and Delbrück hoped that the Copenhagen laboratory would be the place where chemistry and genetics might combine to produce an advance in biology.

Their plan, however, was a complete failure. Herman Kalckar did not manage to interest me at all. I found myself just as bored by nucleic-acid chemistry as I had been in the States. This was

8

partly because I could not see how the type of problem he was working on then would lead to anything of immediate interest to genetics. There was also the fact that, though Herman was obviously civilized, it was impossible to understand him.

I was able, however, to follow the English of Herman's close friend, Ole Maaløe. Ole had just returned from the States (Cal Tech), where he had become very excited about the same bacterial viruses on which I had worked for my degree. On his return he gave up his previous area of work and was now spending all his time on them. Then he was the only Dane working in this area and so was quite pleased that I and Gunther Stent, a bacterial virus worker from Delbrück's laboratory, had come to work with Herman. Soon Gunther and I found ourselves going regularly to visit Ole's laboratory, which was several kilometres from Herman's, and within weeks we were both actively doing experiments with Ole.

At first I occasionally felt uncomfortable about this, because I had been sent to learn biochemistry with Herman. Moreover, less than three months after my arrival in Copenhagen I was asked to propose plans for the following year. This was not a simple matter, as I had no plans. The only safe option was to ask for funds to spend another year with Herman. It would have been risky to say that I could not make myself enjoy biochemistry. Furthermore, I could see no reason why they should not permit me to change my plans after the second year was approved. So I wrote to Washington saying that I wished to remain in Copenhagen. As expected, the money was made available for a second year of study.

I wondered whether Herman minded the fact that I was seldom around. He appeared very unclear about most things and might not yet have really noticed. Fortunately, however, these fears never had time to develop seriously. Through a completely unexpected event, I found I could stop feeling guilty. One day early in December, I cycled over to Herman's laboratory expecting another charming conversation which was impossible to understand. This time, however, I found that things were different. Herman had something important to say: his marriage was over, and he hoped to obtain a divorce. This fact was soon no secret – everyone else in the laboratory was also told. Within a few days it became apparent that Herman's mind was not going to concentrate on science for some time, for perhaps as long as I would remain in Copenhagen. So the fact that he did not have to teach me nucleic-acid biochemistry was obviously a piece of good luck. I could cycle over to Ole's laboratory, knowing it was clearly better to deceive Washington about where I was working than to force Herman to talk about biochemistry.

At times, moreover, I was quite pleased with my experiments on bacterial viruses. Within three months Ole and I had collected enough data for a respectable publication and, using ordinary standards, I knew I could stop work for the rest of the year without being judged unproductive. On the other hand, it was equally obvious that I had not done anything which was going to tell us what a gene was or how it could copy itself. And unless I became a chemist, I could not see how I would.

So I welcomed Herman's suggestion that I should go that spring to an animal study centre in Naples, where he had decided to spend the months of April and May. A trip to Naples made great sense. There was no point in doing nothing in Copenhagen, where spring does not exist. On the other hand, the sun of Naples might encourage me to learn something about the biochemistry of the early development of marine animals. It might also be a place where I could quietly read genetics. And when I was tired of it, I might even pick up a book on biochemistry. Without any hesitation I wrote to the States requesting permission to accompany Herman to Naples. A cheerful letter wishing me a pleasant journey came by return

10

post from Washington. Moreover, it enclosed a two-hundred-dollar cheque for travel expenses. It made me feel slightly dishonest as I set off for the sun.

◆

Maurice Wilkins had also not come to Naples for serious science. The trip from London was an unexpected gift from his boss, J. T. Randall. Originally, Randall had planned to come to the meeting on large molecules and read a paper about the work going on in his new biophysics laboratory. Finding himself too busy, he decided to send Maurice instead. If no one went, it would look bad for his King's College laboratory. Lots of scarce British government money had been spent to set this up, and suspicions existed that this was money wasted.

By the time Maurice arrived, I was noticeably restless and impatient to return north. Herman had completely deceived me. For the first six weeks in Naples I was constantly cold. The official temperature is often much less relevant than the absence of central heating. Neither the animal study centre nor my room on the top floor of a six-storey nineteenth-century house had any heat. If I had had even the slightest interest in marine animals, I would have done experiments. Moving about doing experiments is much warmer than sitting in the library with one's feet on the table. At times I stood about nervously while Herman did some biochemistry, and on several days I even understood what he said. It made no difference, however, whether or not I followed the argument. Genes were never at the centre, or even at the edge, of his thoughts.

Most of my time I spent walking the streets or reading journal articles from the early days of genetics. Sometimes I daydreamed about discovering the secret of the gene, but not once did I have the faintest trace of a respectable idea. It was therefore difficult to avoid the disturbing thought that I was not achieving anything.

11

Knowing that I had not come to Naples for work did not make me feel better.

I still had a slight hope that I might profit from the meeting on the structures of large biological molecules. Though I knew nothing about the X-ray diffraction methods that dominated structural analysis, I was optimistic that the spoken arguments would be easier to understand than the journal articles. I was specially interested to hear the talk on nucleic acids which would be given by Randall. At that time almost nothing was published about the possible shapes of a nucleic-acid molecule, and perhaps this fact affected my relaxed attitude to learning chemistry. Why should I get excited about learning boring chemical facts if the chemists never provided any useful information about the nucleic acids?

The chances, however, were against learning anything new then about the shapes of proteins and nucleic acids. Though this work had been going on for over fifteen years, most if not all of the facts were untested. Ideas put forward with conviction were likely to be the products of wild crystallographers who were delighted to be in a field where their ideas could not easily be disproved. Because of this, although almost all biochemists, including Herman, were unable to understand the arguments of the X-ray people, there was little anxiety. It made no sense to learn complicated mathematical methods in order to understand nonsense. As a result, none of my teachers ever considered the possibility that I might work with an X-ray crystallographer.

Maurice, however, did not disappoint me. The fact that he was there in place of Randall made no difference: I had not known about either of them. His talk stood out sharply from the rest, several of which had no connection to the purpose of the meeting. In contrast, Maurice's X-ray diffraction picture of DNA was relevant. It was shown on the screen towards the end of his talk. Maurice's English voice showed little emotion as he stated that the picture showed much more detail than previous pictures and could, in fact, be considered as that of a crystalline structure. And when the structure of DNA was known, we might be in a better position to understand how genes work.

Suddenly, I was excited about chemistry. Before Maurice's talk I had worried about the possibility that the gene might be completely irregular. Now, however, I knew that genes could crystallize; therefore they must have a regular structure that could be solved in an uncomplicated way. Immediately I began to wonder whether it might be possible for me to join Wilkins in working on DNA. After the lecture I tried to find him. Perhaps he already knew more than his talk had indicated – often if a scientist is not absolutely sure he is correct, he hesitates to speak in public. But there was no opportunity to speak to him. Maurice had disappeared.

Not till the next day, when everybody took a trip to the Greek ruins at Paestum, did I get an opportunity to introduce myself. While waiting for the bus, I started a conversation and explained how interested I was in DNA. But before I could ask any questions the bus arrived, and I sat beside my sister, Elizabeth, who had just come in from the States. At the ruins we scattered, and before I could find Maurice again I realized that I might have had a great piece of good luck. Maurice had noticed that my sister was very pretty, and soon they were eating lunch together. I was very pleased. If Maurice really liked my sister, it was inevitable that I would become involved with his X-ray work on DNA. The fact that he went to sit alone when I arrived did not upset me. He obviously had good manners and assumed that I wished to talk to Elizabeth.

As soon as we reached Naples, however, my daydreams ended. Maurice moved off to his hotel with only a nod of his head. Neither the beauty of my sister nor my interest in DNA had captured him. Our futures did not seem to be in London. And so

13

I set off to Copenhagen again with only the thought of more biochemistry to avoid.

◆

I forgot about Maurice, but not his DNA photograph. This might be a key to the secret of life, and it was impossible to push it out of my mind. The fact that I was unable to understand it did not bother me. It was certainly better to imagine myself becoming famous than growing into a quiet university teacher who had never risked a thought. I was also encouraged by the very exciting rumour that Linus Pauling had partly solved the structure of proteins. The news hit me in Geneva, where I had stopped for several days to talk with the Swiss virologist Jean Weigle, who was just back from a winter at Cal Tech. Before leaving, Jean had gone to a lecture where Linus had made the announcement.

Pauling had talked as if he had been in show business all his life. A curtain kept his model hidden until near the end of his lecture, when he proudly showed off his latest creation. Then, with his eyes shining, Linus explained exactly what made his model – the alpha helix – uniquely beautiful. This show, like all of his performances, delighted the younger students there. Several of the scientists, however, watched with mixed feelings. Seeing Linus jumping up and down and moving his arms like a magician who would soon pull a rabbit out of his shoe made them feel inadequate. If only he had been a little more humble, it would have been so much easier to accept! A number of his colleagues waited quietly for the day when he would fall flat on his face by making a big mistake about something important.

But Jean could not tell me whether Linus's alpha helix was right. He was not an X-ray crystallographer and could not judge the model professionally. Several of his younger friends, however, trained in structural chemistry, thought the alpha helix looked very pretty. Their best guess was that Linus was correct. If so, this was one more highly significant achievement. Linus would be the first person to propose something solidly correct about the structure of a biologically important large molecule. Possibly, he might also have discovered a sensational new method which could be extended to the nucleic acids.

By the time I was back in Copenhagen, a journal containing an article by Linus on the alpha helix had arrived from the States. I quickly read it and immediately reread it. Most of the language was above me, and I could only get a general idea of his argument. I had no way of judging whether it made sense. The only thing I was sure of was that it was written with style.

So I began worrying about where I could learn to understand X-ray diffraction pictures. Cal Tech was not the place – Linus was too great a man to waste his time teaching a biologist with limited mathematics. Neither did I wish to be ignored again by Wilkins. This left Cambridge, England, where I knew that someone named Max Perutz was interested in the structure of the large biological molecules. So I wrote to Luria about my new interest, asking whether he knew how to arrange my acceptance into the Cambridge laboratory. Unexpectedly, this was no problem at all. Soon after receiving my letter, Luria went to a small meeting at Ann Arbor,* where he met Perutz's colleague, John Kendrew, then on an extended trip to the States. Most fortunately, Luria liked Kendrew; he was as civilized as Kalckar and in addition supported the Labour Party. Furthermore, the Cambridge laboratory was understaffed and Kendrew was looking for someone to join him in his study of the proteins. Luria assured him I would be suitable and immediately wrote to tell me the good news.

It was then early August, just a month before my original funding from the States would end. This meant that I could not

*Ann Arbor: a town in Michigan, the main site of the University of Michigan.

delay writing to Washington about my change of plans for much longer. I decided to wait until I was admitted officially into the Cambridge laboratory. There was always the possibility that something would go wrong. Also, I did not want to be away during an approaching international conference, which would bring several bacterial virus workers to Copenhagen. Max Delbrück was in the expected group, and since he was in a senior position at Cal Tech, he might have further news about Pauling's latest trick.

Delbrück, however, could tell me nothing more. The alpha helix, even if correct, had not provided any new biological knowledge; he seemed quite bored speaking about it. But I had no opportunity to be depressed by his lack of enthusiasm, because the conference was a huge success. From the moment the several hundred scientists arrived, a great amount of free drink, partly provided by American dollars, was available to improve international relations. Each night there were parties, dinners and midnight trips to waterside bars. An important truth was slowly entering my head: a scientist's life might be interesting socially as well as intellectually. I went off to England in a very good mood.

Chapter 3   Making a Start

Max Perutz was in his office when I came in just after lunch. John Kendrew was still in the States, but my arrival was not unexpected. A brief letter from John said that an American biologist might work with him during the following year. I explained that I had no knowledge of how X-rays diffract, but Max immediately made me feel comfortable. I was told that no advanced mathematics would be required. All I had to do was read a book on crystallography; this would give me enough theory to begin to take X-ray photographs. As an example, Max told me about how he had tested Pauling's alpha helix. Only a day had been required to get the important photograph confirming Pauling's prediction. I did not understand what Max was saying at all. I did not even know about Bragg's Law, the most basic of all crystallographic ideas.

We then went for a walk to look at possible accommodation for the coming year. When Max realized that I had come directly to the laboratory from the station and had not yet seen any of the colleges, he changed direction to take me through King's and along the side of the river to Trinity College. I had never seen such beautiful buildings in all my life, and any hesitation I might have had about my safe life as a biologist disappeared. Because of this I was only slightly depressed when I looked inside several houses which contained student rooms. In the end, I thought myself very lucky when I found a room in a two-storey house on Jesus Green, less than ten minutes' walk from the laboratory.

The following morning I went back to the Cavendish, since Max wanted me to meet Sir Lawrence Bragg. Bragg came down from his office, let me say a few words, and then went off for a private conversation with Max. A few minutes later, they came out to allow Bragg to give me his formal permission to work under his direction. The performance was typically British, and I quietly decided that the white-moustached figure of Bragg now spent most of his days sitting in London clubs.

The thought never occurred to me then that later on I would have contact with this strange figure from the past. Despite his great reputation, Bragg had worked out his Law before the First World War, so I assumed he must be more or less retired and would never care about genes. I politely thanked Sir Lawrence for accepting me and told Max I would be back in three weeks for the start of term. I then returned to Copenhagen to collect a few clothes and to tell Herman about my good luck in being able to become a crystallographer. Herman sent a letter to Washington in which he enthusiastically approved of my change of plans. At the same time I wrote a letter myself saying that I wanted to give up standard biochemistry, which I believed was incapable of telling us how genes work. Instead, I told them that I now knew that X-ray crystallography was the key to genetics, and asked for approval of my plans to transfer to Perutz's laboratory in Cambridge.

I saw no reason to remain in Copenhagen until permission came. The week before, Maaløe had departed for a year at Cal Tech, and I still had no interest in Herman's type of biochemistry. Also, everyone knew of Herman's unhappy state and his absence from the laboratory, and the Washington office must have been wondering how long I would want to remain there.

In spite of all this, ten days after my return to Cambridge, Herman forwarded bad news, which had been sent to my Copenhagen address. In it, the Washington board told me to reconsider my plans, since I was unqualified to do any crystallographic work.

The source of the trouble was quite obvious. The head of the board was no longer Hans Clarke, a biochemist friend of Herman's, then planning to retire from Columbia. My letter had gone instead to a new chairman, who took a more active interest in directing young people. He was offended that I had said I would not profit from biochemistry. I wrote to Luria to save me. He and the new man knew each other a little, and more details from him might lead to a change of mind.

At first I was cheered up when a letter arrived from Luria saying that the situation might be improved if we appeared very humble and apologetic. I should write to Washington saying that a major reason why I wanted to be in Cambridge was the presence of Roy Markham, an English biochemist who worked with plant viruses. Markham was quite relaxed when I told him he might acquire a good student who would never bother him by doing experiments in his laboratory. He saw the plan as a perfect example of the inability of Americans to know how to behave. However, he agreed to it.

Knowing that Markham would not give me away, I wrote a long letter to Washington, describing how I might profit from working with both Perutz and Markham. At the end I told them honestly that I was in Cambridge and would remain there until a decision was made. The new man in Washington, however, did not cooperate. The clue came when the return letter was addressed to Herman's laboratory. The board was considering my case. I would be informed when a decision had been made. Because of this, it did not seem sensible to cash my cheques, which were still sent to Copenhagen each month.

Fortunately, the possibility of not being paid in the following year for working on DNA was only annoying and not fatal. The three thousand dollars that I had received for being in Copenhagen was three times the amount that a Danish student required to live well. Even if I had to pay for my sister's recent purchase of two fashionable Paris suits, I would have a thousand left, enough for a year's stay in Cambridge. My landlady was also helpful. She threw me out after less than a month. My main crime was not removing my shoes when I entered the house after nine o'clock, the hour at which her husband went to sleep. Even worse, I sometimes went out after ten o'clock. Nothing in Cambridge was open at that time, and my motives were seen as suspicious. John and Elizabeth Kendrew rescued me with the offer, at almost no rent, of a tiny room in their house. It was unbelievably damp and heated only by an ancient electric fire, but I eagerly accepted. Though it looked like an open invitation to serious illness, living with friends was greatly preferable to any other accommodation I might find at this late date.

◆

From my first day in the laboratory I knew that I would not leave Cambridge for a long time. Departing would be silly, because I had immediately discovered the fun of talking to Francis Crick. Finding someone in Max's laboratory who knew that DNA was more important than proteins was real luck. Moreover, it was a great relief for me not to spend all my time learning X-ray analysis of proteins. Our lunch conversations quickly centred on how genes were put together. Within a few days after my arrival, we knew what to do: imitate Linus Pauling and beat him at his own game.

Pauling's success had naturally suggested to Francis that the same tricks might also work for DNA. As long as nobody in Cambridge thought DNA was very important, the possible personal difficulties with the King's laboratory had prevented him from working on it. But now, with me around the laboratory always wanting to talk about genes, Francis began to think about DNA more often.

Because of this, John Kendrew soon realized that I was unlikely to help him with his work on protein structure. Since he was unable to grow large protein crystals, he had hoped that I might be able to help. However, my laboratory work was not very good, and my attempts at crystallization were no more successful than John's. In a way, I was almost relieved. If I had succeeded, he might have told me to take X-ray photographs.

So nothing prevented me from talking at least several hours each day to Francis. Thinking all the time was too much even for Francis, and often when he was puzzled by his calculations he would ask me to tell him about bacterial viruses. At other moments, Francis would try to fill my brain with crystallographic facts. The only other way to learn these would be through slow and painful reading of professional journals. Particularly important were the exact arguments needed to understand how Linus Pauling had discovered the alpha helix.

I was soon taught that Pauling's achievement was a product of common sense, not the result of complicated mathematics. Calculations sometimes came into his arguments, but in most cases words would have been enough. The key to Linus's success was that he relied on the simple laws of structural chemistry. The alpha helix had not been found by only staring at X-ray pictures; the essential trick, instead, was to ask which atoms like to sit next to each other. In place of pencil and paper, the main working tools were a set of molecular models which looked a little like the toys of very young children.

We could therefore see no reason why we should not solve DNA in the same way. All we had to do was to construct a set of molecular models and begin to play — with luck, the structure would be a helix. Any other type of arrangement would be much more complicated.

From our first conversations, we assumed that the DNA molecule contained a very large number of nucleotides linked together in a regular chain. Again, our ideas were partly based on simplicity. Although organic chemists in Alexander Todd's nearby laboratory thought that this was the basic arrangement, they were still a long way from proving that all the bonds between the nucleotides were the same. If this was not the case, however, we could not see how the DNA molecules came together to form the crystalline material studied by Maurice Wilkins and Rosalind Franklin. So, for the moment, the best way forward was to regard the sugar-phosphate backbone as extremely regular and to search for a helical arrangement in which all the backbone groups had the same chemical environment.

Immediately we could see that the solution to DNA would be more tricky than that of the alpha helix. In this, a single chain folds up into a helical arrangement held together by hydrogen bonds between groups on the same chain. Maurice had told Francis, however, that the DNA molecule was thicker than one

21

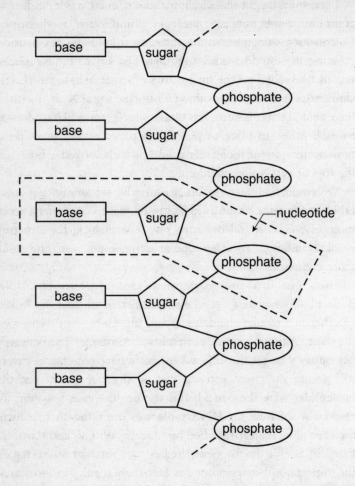

A short section of DNA as imagined by Alexander Todd's group in 1951. They thought that all the links between the nucleotides were made by the phosphates joining with carbon atoms in the sugar molecules. As organic chemists they were concerned with how the atoms were linked together, leaving to crystallographers the problem of the physical shape of the chain.

nucleotide chain. This made him think that the DNA molecule was a complex helix made up of several nucleotide chains twisted around each other. If this was true, then before serious model building began, we would have to decide whether the chains would be held together by hydrogen bonds or by salt bridges involving the negatively charged phosphate groups.

A further complication was that four types of nucleotides were found in DNA. In this sense, DNA was not a regular molecule but an extremely irregular one. The four nucleotides were not, however, completely different, because each contained the same sugar and phosphate parts. Their uniqueness lay in their bases, which were either a purine (of type A or G) or a pyrimidine (type C or T). But since the links between the nucleotides only involved the sugar and phosphate groups, our assumption that the same kind of chemical bond linked all the nucleotides together was not affected. So in building models we would accept that the sugar-phosphate backbone was very regular, and the order of the bases must be very irregular. If the order of the bases was always the same, all DNA molecules would be the same and there would not be the variety that makes one gene different from another.

Though Pauling had found the alpha helix almost without using X-ray data, he knew about it and had included it in his thinking. Because of the X-ray data, a large number of possible arrangements for his chain of structures were quickly excluded. The exact X-ray data should help us go ahead much faster with the complex construction of the DNA molecule. Just looking at the DNA X-ray picture should prevent a number of false starts. Fortunately, one half-good photograph had already been published. It had been taken five years previously by the English crystallographer W. T. Astbury, and could be used to start us off. But having Maurice's much better crystalline photographs might save us from six months to a year's work. We knew we had to talk to him. To our surprise, Francis had no problem in persuading

PURINES

PYRIMIDINES

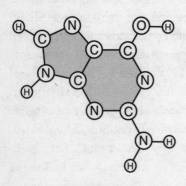

adenine

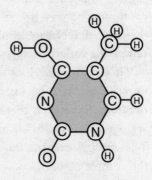

cytosine

guanine

thymine

The chemical structures of the four DNA bases as they were often drawn in about 1951.

Maurice to come up to Cambridge for a weekend. And there was no need to force Maurice to the conclusion that the structure was a helix. Not only was it the obvious guess, but Maurice had already been talking about helices at a summer meeting in Cambridge. About six weeks before I arrived there, he had shown X-ray diffraction pictures of DNA and suggested that it had a helical shape made up of three nucleotide chains.

He did not, however, share our belief that Pauling's model-building game would quickly solve the structure, at least not until further X-ray results were obtained. Most of our conversation, instead, was about Rosy. More trouble than ever was coming from her. She was now insisting that not even Maurice himself should take any more X-ray photographs of DNA. In trying to reach agreement with Rosy, Maurice had made a very bad bargain. He had handed over to her all the good crystalline DNA used in his original work and had agreed to limit his studies to other DNA, which he afterwards found did not crystallize.

The point had been reached where Rosy would not even tell Maurice her latest results. The soonest Maurice was likely to learn what progress she had made was three weeks ahead, the middle of November. At that time Rosy was due to give a talk on her past six months' work. Naturally, I was delighted when Maurice said I would be welcome at this talk. For the first time I had a real reason to learn some crystallography: I wanted to understand what Rosy said.

Chapter 4   The Cochran–Crick Theory

Most unexpectedly, Francis temporarily lost all interest in DNA less than a week later. The reason was his decision to accuse a colleague of ignoring his ideas. It happened less than a month after my arrival, on a Saturday morning. The previous day Max

Perutz had given Francis a new article written by Sir Lawrence and himself, dealing with the shape of a protein molecule. As he quickly read through it Francis became very angry, because he noticed that part of the argument depended upon an idea he had suggested nine months earlier. What was worse, Francis remembered telling it to everyone in the laboratory. But his idea had not been mentioned in the article. Almost at once, after rushing in to tell Max and John Kendrew about this insult, he hurried to Bragg's office for an explanation, if not an apology. But by then Bragg was at home, and Francis had to wait until the following morning. Unfortunately, this delay did not make the meeting any more successful.

Sir Lawrence denied having known anything about Francis's efforts and was extremely insulted by the suggestion that he had secretly used another scientist's ideas. On the other hand, Francis found it impossible to believe that Bragg could have been stupid enough to have missed his idea, which he had talked about many times, and he suggested this very strongly. More conversation became impossible, and in less than ten minutes Francis was out of Bragg's office.

For Bragg, this meeting seemed the end of any good relations with Crick. Several weeks earlier Bragg had come into the laboratory greatly excited about an idea that he had had the previous evening, one that he and Perutz later included in their article. While he was explaining it to Perutz and Kendrew, Crick joined the group. To his great annoyance, Francis did not accept the idea immediately but instead said that he would go away and check whether Bragg was right or wrong. At that point Bragg had become very angry.

This most recent argument was a disaster for Francis, and he looked worried when he came down to the laboratory. Bragg, when he sent him out of his room, had angrily told him that he would consider seriously whether he could continue to give

Francis a place in the laboratory after his Ph.D course was ended. Francis was obviously worried that he might have to find a new position.

His worry was not without a good reason. Although he knew that he was clever and could produce new ideas, he could claim no obvious intellectual achievements, and he was still without his Ph.D. He came from a solid middle-class family, studied physics at University College, London, and had started work on an advanced degree when the war began. Like almost all other English scientists, he joined the war effort and became part of the navy's scientific team. He worked with great energy, and, although many disliked his non-stop conversation, there was a war to win and he was quite helpful in producing new weapons. When the war was over, however, some of his colleagues saw no good reason to have him around forever, and he learned that he had no future in the government scientific service.

Moreover, he had lost all desire to stay in physics and decided instead to try biology. He managed to get a small amount of money to come to Cambridge in the autumn of 1947. At first he did pure biology, but two years later he moved over to the Cavendish. Here he again became excited about science and decided that he should finally work for a Ph.D. So he became a student (of Caius College), studying under Max. In a way, Ph.D work was boring for a mind that worked so fast, but his decision had produced an unexpected advantage: in this difficult time, he would not be sent away before he got his degree.

Max and John came quickly to Francis's rescue and spoke to Bragg. John confirmed that Francis had previously written about this argument, and Bragg accepted that the same idea had come independently to both of them. Bragg by that time had calmed down, and the idea of Crick going was quietly dropped. Keeping him was not easy for Bragg. One day, in a moment of unhappiness, he revealed that Crick made his ears ring. Moreover, he still could not believe that Crick was needed. For thirty-five years Crick had not stopped talking, but he had said almost nothing of real value.

◆

A new opportunity to think about theory soon brought Francis back to normal. Several days after the problem with Bragg, the crystallographer V. Vand sent Max a letter containing a theory for the diffraction of X-rays by helical molecules. Helices were then at the centre of the laboratory's interest, mainly because of Pauling's alpha helix. But there was still no general theory to test new models as well as to confirm the details of the alpha helix. This is what Vand hoped his theory would do.

Francis quickly found a serious fault in Vand's efforts, became excited about finding the right theory, and ran upstairs to talk with Bill Cochran, a small, quiet Scot, then a lecturer in crystallography at the Cavendish. Bill was the cleverest of the younger Cambridge X-ray people and the best person for Francis to discuss his many new theories with. When Bill told Francis that an idea would not work or would lead nowhere, Francis could be sure that professional jealousy was not involved. This time, however, Bill did not disagree with Francis, because he had also found faults in Vand's paper and had begun to wonder what the right answer was. For months both Max and Bragg had been asking him to work out the helical theory, but he had not moved into action. Now, with additional pressure from Francis, he too had begun seriously to think about the mathematics.

For the rest of the morning Francis was silent because he was also thinking about mathematics. Then at lunchtime he got a bad headache and he went home. But sitting in front of his gas fire doing nothing bored him, and he started on the mathematics again. To his delight, he soon saw that he had the answer. However, he stopped his work because he and his wife, Odile, were invited to a wine tasting at Matthews', one of the better Cambridge shops. For several days he had been looking forward to this. It meant acceptance by a more fashionable and amusing part of Cambridge and allowed him to forget that he was not appreciated by a variety of dull and self-important university people.

He and Odile were then living at the 'Green Door', a tiny inexpensive flat on top of a several-hundred-year-old house just across Bridge Street from St John's College. There were only two real rooms, a living room and a bedroom. All the others, including the kitchen, in which the bath was the largest and most visible object, were almost non-existent. But despite the small size, its great charm (increased by Odile's decorative sense) made it a cheerful and happy place. Here I first sensed the energy of English intellectual life, so completely absent during my first days in my room several hundred metres away.

They had been married for three years. Francis's first marriage did not last long, and a son, Michael, was looked after by Francis's mother and aunt. He had lived alone for several years until Odile, five years younger than him, came to Cambridge. She shared his dislike of the dullness of the middle classes, which enjoy healthy amusements like sailing and tennis, habits particularly unsuited to a conversational life.

By then I was often going to the Green Door for dinner. Francis was always eager to continue our conversations, while I joyously seized every opportunity to escape from the miserable English food that frequently made me wonder if I had a stomach problem. Odile's French mother had given her a strong dislike for the way in which most Englishmen eat and house themselves. Because of this, Francis never had reason to envy those lecturers whose college food was much better than their wives' boring mixtures of tasteless meat, boiled potatoes, colourless vegetables and typical puddings. Instead, dinner was often happy, especially after the wine turned the conversation to the more attractive women of Cambridge.

But there were no young women at the wine tasting. To his and Odile's disappointment, their companions were college lecturers talking about the burden of paperwork which they had to cope with. They went home early and Francis, who had drunk less than usual, thought more about his answer.

The next morning he arrived at the laboratory and told Max and John about his success. A few minutes later, Bill Cochran walked into his office, and Francis started to repeat the story. But then Bill told him that he also thought he had succeeded. Quickly they each went through their mathematics and discovered that Bill's version was shorter and more elegant than Francis's. Happily, however, they found that they had arrived at the same final answer. They then checked the alpha helix by visual inspection with Max's X-ray diagrams. The agreement was so good that both Linus's model and the theory had to be correct.

Within a few days, a finished article was ready and sent off to *Nature*. At the same time, a copy was sent to Pauling to appreciate. This event, his first unquestionable success, was a great thing for Francis. This time the absence of women had been accompanied by luck.

Chapter 5   Rosy's Results

By mid-November, the time of Rosy's talk on DNA, I had learned enough about crystallography to understand much of her lecture. Most importantly, I knew which parts to give my attention to. After six weeks of listening to Francis, I knew that what really mattered was whether Rosy's new X-ray pictures would give   any support to a helical DNA structure. The really relevant experimental details were those which might provide clues in constructing molecular models. It took, however, only a few minutes of listening to Rosy to realize that her determined mind had decided on a different course of action.

She spoke to an audience of about fifteen in a quick, nervous style. There was not a trace of warmth or lightness in her words. Even so, I could not regard her as totally uninteresting. For a moment, I wondered how she would look if she took off her glasses and did something different with her hair. Then, however, my interest moved back to her description of the crystalline X-ray diffraction pattern.

The years of careful, unemotional crystallographic training had left their mark. It was totally obvious to her that the only way to discover the DNA structure was by a pure crystallographic method. As model building did not appeal to her, at no time did she mention Pauling's success over the alpha helix. The idea of using toy-like models to solve biological structures was clearly last on her list of possible ways forward. Of course Rosy knew of Linus's success, but she saw no obvious reason to copy his methods. The record of his past victories was enough of a reason to act differently; only someone as brilliant as Linus could play like a ten-year-old boy and still get the right answer.

Rosy regarded her talk as an initial report which, by itself, would not test anything basic about DNA. Hard facts would only come when further data had been collected which could allow the crystallographic analyses to move to a more advanced stage. The small group of laboratory people who came to the talk appeared no more optimistic. No one else spoke about the desirability of using molecular models to help solve the structure. Maurice himself only asked several questions of a technical nature. The discussion then quickly stopped. Maybe the unwillingness of the others to say anything optimistic, or even to mention models, was due to fear of a sharp response from Rosy.

Following some brief and typically tense conversation with Rosy, Maurice and I walked to a Soho restaurant. Maurice's mood was surprisingly cheerful. Slowly and exactly, he explained how, in spite of much complex crystallographic analysis, little real progress had been made by Rosy since the day she arrived at King's. Though her X-ray photographs were a little sharper than his, she was unable to say anything more positive than he had already. She had done some more detailed analysis of the amount of water in DNA, but even here Maurice had doubts about whether she was really measuring what she claimed.

To my surprise, Maurice seemed happy to be in my company. The shyness that existed when we first met in Naples had disappeared. He seemed to appreciate the fact that I, one of the bacterial virus group, found what he was doing important. It really was no help to receive encouragement from another physicist. Even when he met those who thought his decision to go into biology made sense, he could not trust their judgement. After all, they did not know any biology, and so it was best to take their remarks as politeness towards someone opposed to the competitive speed of post-war physics.

He did get active and very necessary help from some biochemists. If not, he could never have come into the game. Several of them had helped a great deal in providing him with some highly purified DNA. On the other hand, the majority were not like the ambitious types he had worked with on the atomic bomb project. Sometimes they did not even seem to know why DNA was important.

So the knowledge that the bacterial virus group took DNA seriously made Maurice hope that times would change and he would not have to explain, each time he gave a talk, why his laboratory was making so much noise about DNA. By the time our dinner was finished, he was clearly in a mood to push ahead. But then Rosy came back into the conversation, and the possibility of really getting the laboratory moving forward grew less and less as we paid the bill and went out into the night.

◆

The following morning I joined Francis at Paddington Station. From there we were going up to Oxford to spend the weekend. Francis wanted to talk to Dorothy Hodgkin, the best of the English crystallographers, while I welcomed the opportunity to see Oxford for the first time. At the station, Francis seemed very happy. The visit would give him the chance to tell Dorothy about his success with Bill Cochran in working out the helical diffraction theory. The theory was much too elegant not to be told in person – those like Dorothy who were clever enough to understand its power immediately were much too rare.

As soon as we were in the train carriage, Francis began asking questions about Rosy's talk. My answers were frequently unclear, and Francis was visibly annoyed by my habit of always trusting to memory and never writing anything on paper. If a subject interested me, I could usually remember what I needed. This time, however, we were in trouble, because I did not know enough of the crystallographic vocabulary. Particularly unfortunate was my failure to be able to report exactly the amount of water in the DNA upon which Rosy had done her measurements. It was possible that I might be deceiving Francis by a difference of ten times the figures she gave.

The wrong person had been sent to hear Rosy. If Francis had gone along, he would have written everything down. It was the penalty for being oversensitive to the situation. Certainly, the sight of Francis thinking about the consequences of Rosy's information when it was hardly out of her mouth would have upset Maurice. In one way, it would be highly unfair for them to learn the facts at the same time. Certainly, Maurice should have the first chance to work on the problem. On the other hand, there seemed no indication that he thought the answer would come from playing with molecular models. Our conversation the previous night had hardly mentioned that approach. Of course, the possibility existed that he was keeping something back. But that was very unlikely – Maurice just was not that type.

The only thing Francis could do immediately was to seize the water value, which was easiest to think about. Soon something appeared to make sense, and he began to write on the blank back sheet of an article he had been reading. By then I could not understand what Francis was doing, and opened *The Times* for amusement. Within a few minutes, however, Francis made me lose all interest in the outside world by telling me that only a small number of structures were possible according to both the Cochran–Crick theory and Rosy's experimental data. Quickly he began to draw more diagrams to show me how simple the problem was. Though the mathematics was too difficult for me, the important part was not difficult to understand. Decisions had to be made about the number of nucleotide chains within the DNA molecule. The X-ray data, as we understood it, would allow for two, three or four chains. It was all a question of the angle of twist and the distance apart of the chains.

By the time the hour-and-a-half train journey was over, Francis saw no reason why we should not know the answer soon. Perhaps a week of playing with the molecular models would be necessary to make us absolutely sure we had the right answer. Then it would be obvious to the world that Pauling was not the only one capable of really understanding how biological molecules were constructed. Linus's capture of the alpha helix was most embarrassing for the Cambridge group. About a year before that success, Bragg, Kendrew and Perutz had published a paper on the structure of the chains that Linus was working with. It showed a misunderstanding of the situation and Bragg was still bothered by that failure. There had been previous struggles with

Linus, stretching back over a twenty-five-year period. Most times, Linus had got there first.

Even Francis was a little embarrassed by the event. He had been present at a discussion in which the basic mistake about the shape of the bonds in the chain had been made. That had certainly been the right occasion to use his ability to assess the meaning of experimental observations – but he had said nothing useful. Francis did not normally hold back from criticizing his friends. In other situations he had been annoyingly honest in pointing out where Perutz and Bragg had publicly misread their results. This open criticism was certainly behind Sir Lawrence's recent anger with him. In Bragg's view, all Crick did was to upset people.

Now, however, was not the time to concentrate on past mistakes. Instead, the speed with which we talked about possible types of DNA structures increased as the morning went by. Whenever we found ourselves with a new companion, Francis would quickly look back over the progress of the past few hours, bringing our listener up to date on how we had decided on models in which the sugar-phosphate backbone was in the centre of the molecule. Only in that way would it be possible to obtain a structure regular enough to give the crystalline diffraction patterns observed by Maurice and Rosy. We still had to deal with the irregular order of the bases that faced the outside – but this difficulty might disappear when the correct internal arrangement was found.

There was also the problem of what neutralized the negative charge of the phosphate groups of the DNA backbone. Francis, as well as I, knew almost nothing about how inorganic ions were arranged in actual space. We had to face the difficult situation that the world authority on the structural chemistry of ions was Linus Pauling himself. Because of this, if the main part of the problem was to work out a clever arrangement of inorganic ions and

35

phosphate groups, we were clearly at a disadvantage. By midday it became very important to find a copy of Linus's book on the subject. We were having lunch but, wasting no time over coffee, we ran into several bookshops until success came in Blackwell's. We quickly read the relevant sections. This produced the correct values for the exact sizes of the important inorganic ions, but nothing that could really help to solve the problem.

When we reached Dorothy's laboratory in the University Museum, we had slowed down a little. Francis talked through the helical theory itself, giving only a few minutes to our progress with DNA. Most of the conversation was about Dorothy's recent work in other areas. Since darkness was coming, there seemed no point in wasting more of her time. We then moved on to Magdalen College, where we had tea with Avrion Mitchison and Leslie Orgel. Over cakes Francis was ready to talk about small things, while I quietly thought how splendid it would be if I could some day live in the style of a Magdalen lecturer.

Chapter 6   First Attempt

I told John and Elizabeth Kendrew the news about our progress with DNA when I joined them for breakfast on Monday morning. Elizabeth appeared delighted that success was almost within our reach, while John took the news more calmly. When he realized that I had nothing more solid to report than enthusiasm, his attention turned to *The Times*. Soon afterwards, John went off to his rooms at Peterhouse College, leaving Elizabeth and me to think about my unexpected luck. I did not remain long, since the sooner I could get back to the laboratory, the quicker we could find out which of the several possible answers would be suggested by a hard look at the molecular models themselves.

Both Francis and I, however, knew that the models in the Cavendish would not be completely satisfactory. They had been put together by John about eighteen months before, for the work on the shape of the chain that Linus had solved. There existed no accurate representation of the groups of atoms unique to DNA. Neither phosphorus atoms nor the purine and pyrimidine bases were available. We would have to make these ourselves. Having completely new models made might take a week, while an answer was possible within a day or two. So as soon as I got to the laboratory, I started adding bits of wire to some of our carbon-atom models, in this way changing them into the larger-sized phosphorus atoms.

Much more difficulty came from the need to build models of the inorganic ions. Unlike the other parts, they obeyed no simple rules telling us the angles at which they would form their chemical bonds. Most likely we had to know the correct DNA structure before the right models could be made. I maintained the hope, however, that Francis might already have worked out an answer. Over eighteen hours had passed since our last conversation, and there was little chance that he would have been interested in the Sunday papers after his return to the Green Door.

His entrance at about ten o'clock, however, did not bring the answer. After Sunday supper he had again thought about the problem but saw no quick answer. But over morning coffee he seemed confident that enough experimental data might already be available to determine the correct way forward. We might be able to start the game with several completely different sets of facts and still always hit the final answers. Perhaps the whole problem would solve itself by concentrating on the prettiest way for a nucleotide chain to fold up. So while Francis continued thinking about the meaning of the X-ray diagram, I began to put the various atomic models into several chains, each several nucleotides in length. Though in nature DNA chains are very long, there was no reason to put together anything massive. If we could be sure it was a helix, the assignment of the positions for only a couple of nucleotides automatically determined the arrangement of all the other parts.

The routine assembly task was over by one, when Francis and I walked over to a nearby pub for our habitual lunch with the chemist Herbert Gutfreund. When we walked in, Francis did not exchange his usual noisy greetings with the Persian economist Ephraim Eshag, but instead gave the impression that something serious was on his mind. The actual model-building would start right after lunch, and more definite plans must be made to make the process more efficient. So over our fruit pie we considered the advantages and disadvantages of one, two, three and four chains, quickly dismissing one-chain helices as being against the evidence that we had. The best guess for forces that held the chains together seemed to be salt bridges holding together two or more phosphate groups. There was no evidence for this in the results that Rosy had obtained, so we might be taking a chance. On the other hand, there was no reason to believe we might not be right. If only the King's group had thought about models, they would have asked which salt was present and we would not have been placed in this annoying position.

Our first minutes with the models, though, were not joyous. Although only about fifteen atoms were involved, they kept falling out of the awkward connectors set up to hold them the correct distance from one another. Even worse, we began to get the uncomfortable impression that there were no obvious limits to the bond angles between several of the most important atoms. This was not at all nice. Pauling had worked out the alpha helix from his knowledge that the bond he was dealing with was flat. To our annoyance, there seemed every reason to believe that the bonds which held together the neighbouring nucleotides of DNA might exist in a variety of shapes. At least with our level of chemical knowledge, there was unlikely to be any single structure much prettier than the rest.

After tea, however, a shape began to appear which raised our spirits. Three chains twisted around each other in a way that gave rise to a regular crystallographic repeat every 28 hundred-millionths of a centimetre. This was a feature demanded by Maurice's and Rosy's pictures, so Francis seemed more confident when he stepped back from the laboratory table and surveyed the afternoon's effort. It was true that a few of the atomic contacts were still too close, but the delicate work had just begun. After a few more hours, a presentable model should be on display.

We were both cheerful during the evening meal at the Green Door. Though Odile could not understand what we were saying, she was obviously happy that Francis was going to have his second success within the month. If events continued in this way, they would soon be rich and could own a car. At no moment did Francis see any reason to simplify the matter for Odile's benefit. This part of their relationship was fixed. She did not know any science and seemed uninterested in learning any.

Our conversation instead centred on a young art student who was going to marry Odile's friend Harmut Weil. This capture was mildly displeasing to Francis. It would remove the prettiest girl from their party group.

There was no thought of women, however, when Francis marched into the laboratory just before morning coffee. Soon, when several atoms had been pushed in or out, the three-chain model began to look quite reasonable. The next obvious step would be to check it with Rosy's measurements. The model would certainly fit with the general positions of the X-ray reflections, because its essential helical shape had been chosen to fit the facts from Rosy's talk that I had passed on to Francis. If it were right, however, the model would also accurately predict the strengths of the various X-ray reflections in relation to each other.

A quick phone call was made to Maurice. Francis explained how the helical diffraction theory allowed a rapid assessment of possible DNA models, and that he and I had thought of one which might be the answer we were all waiting for. The best thing would be for Maurice to come and look at it. But Maurice gave no definite date, saying he thought he might manage some time within the week. Soon after the phone was put down, John came in to see how Maurice had taken our news. Francis found it hard to form his reply. It was almost as if Maurice did not care about what we were doing.

In the middle of further work on the model that afternoon, a call came through from King's. Maurice would come up on the 10.10 train from London the following morning. Moreover, he would not be alone. His colleague Willy Seeds would also come. Even more interesting was that Rosy and her student R. G. Gosling, would be on the same train. Apparently they were still interested in the answer.

◆

Maurice decided to take a taxi from the station to the laboratory. Normally he would have come by bus, but there would be no satisfaction in waiting at the bus stop with Rosy. His attempts to have a conversation with her were all failures, and even now, when the possibility of being proved wrong hung over them, Rosy still ignored him and directed all her attention to Gosling. Only the slightest effort at a united appearance was made when Maurice put his head into our laboratory to say they had come.

Francis and I had earlier agreed to reveal our progress in two stages. Francis would first summarize the advantages of the helical theory. Then together we would explain how we had arrived at the proposed model for DNA. Afterwards we could go to the Eagle for lunch, leaving the afternoon free to discuss how we would proceed with the final phases of the problem.

The first part of the show went according to plan. Francis saw no reason to be cautious about describing the power of the helical theory and within several minutes revealed how it gave neat answers. None of the visitors, however, showed any sign of sharing Francis's delight. Instead of wishing to do something with the theory, Maurice wanted to concentrate on the fact that it did not go beyond some mathematics that his colleague Stokes had worked out without all this display. Stokes had solved the problem in the train while going home one evening and had produced the theory on a small sheet of paper the next morning.

Rosy did not care at all about who first created the helical theory and, as Francis talked on, she displayed growing impatience. The lesson was unnecessary, since to her mind there was no evidence that DNA was helical. Whether this was correct would come out of further X-ray work. Inspection of the model itself only increased her opposition. She even became aggressive when we reached the topic of the positive ions which held together the phosphate groups of our three-chain model. This feature had no appeal at all to Rosy, who coldly pointed out that the ions would be surrounded by tight shells of water molecules and so were unlikely to be the key parts of a tight structure.

Most annoyingly, her objections did not just come from her attempts to be difficult: at this stage the embarrassing fact came out that my memory of the amount of water in the DNA Rosy worked with could not be right. The awkward truth became clear that the correct DNA model must contain at least ten times more water than was found in our model. This did not mean that we were definitely wrong – with luck we might be able to place the water in vacant areas on the edge of our helix. On the other hand, we could not escape the conclusion that our argument was weak. As soon as we accepted that much more water might be involved, the number of possible DNA models increased alarmingly.

Though Francis could not help dominating the lunchtime conversation, his mood was no longer confident. It was clear to all which group had won the argument. The best way to rescue something from the day was to come to an agreement about the next set of experiments. In particular, only a few weeks' work should be necessary to see whether the DNA structure depended on the exact ions used to neutralize the negative phosphate groups. With this achieved, another period of model-building could start, perhaps before Christmas.

Our after-lunch walk into King's and along the riverside to Trinity did not, however, reveal any movement towards our point of view. Rosy and Gosling were still in a fighting mood; their future course of action would not be affected by their eighty-kilometre journey into youthful nonsense. Maurice and Willy Seeds gave more indication of being reasonable, but there was no certainty that this was not simply because they did not want to agree with Rosy.

The situation did not improve when we got back to the laboratory. Francis did not want to surrender immediately, so he talked through some of the actual details of how we had done the model-building. However, he quickly lost his enthusiasm when it became apparent that I was the only one joining the conversation. Moreover, by this time neither of us really wanted to look at our model. All its charm had disappeared, and the home-made phosphorus atoms gave no indication that they would ever fit neatly into something of value. Then when Maurice mentioned that, if they moved quickly, they might catch the 3.40 train to Liverpool Street Station, we quickly said goodbye.

◆

Bragg soon learned of Rosy's great victory. We could only appear untroubled as the news confirmed the fact that Francis might move faster if occasionally he would close his mouth. The consequences spread in a predictable way. Clearly this was the moment for Maurice's boss to discuss with Bragg whether it made sense for Crick and the American to do the same kind of work as King's was putting so much effort into.

Sir Lawrence had had too much of Francis to be surprised that he had again caused unnecessary trouble. There was no way of knowing where Francis would set off the next explosion. If he continued to behave this way, he could easily spend five years in the laboratory without collecting enough data to deserve an honest Ph.D. The frightening thought of having to put up with Francis during his remaining years in charge of the Cavendish was too much to ask of Bragg or anyone with a normal set of nerves.

The decision was therefore passed on to Max that Francis and I must give up DNA. Bragg had no fears that this would hold back science, since inquiries to Max and John had revealed nothing original in our approach. After Pauling's success, no one could be blamed for believing in helices. Letting the King's group have the first attempt at helical models was the right thing in any situation. Crick could then get on with his Ph.D task of investigating the way that certain protein crystals shrink when they are placed in salt solutions of different strengths. A year to eighteen months of steady work might tell something more solid about the shape of various protein molecules. With a Ph.D in his pocket, Crick could then seek employment elsewhere.

No attempt was made to appeal against this decision. To the relief of Max and John, we did not publicly question it. An open protest would reveal that our boss was completely unaware of what the initials DNA stood for. Our acceptance of all this did not come, however, from a desire to keep peace with Bragg. Staying quiet made sense because we were in deep trouble with models based on sugar-phosphate backbones. No matter how we looked at them, they did not seem right. On the day following the visit from King's, we looked carefully at both the unfortunate three-chain model and a number of possible alternatives. We could not be sure, but we had the impression that any model placing the sugar–phosphate backbone in the centre of a helix forced atoms closer together than the laws of chemistry allowed. Positioning one atom the proper distance from its neighbour often caused a distant atom to be placed impossibly close to its partners.

A new start would be necessary to get the problem moving again. Sadly, however, we realized that our suddenly spoiled relationship with King's would remove our source of new experimental results. Further invitations to talks on their work were not to be expected, and any questioning of Maurice would make him suspicious that we had returned to the problem. What was worse was the almost total certainty that they would not start to build models now that we had stopped. To our knowledge, King's had not built any models of the necessary atoms. Our offer to speed up that task by giving them the Cambridge equipment for making the models was not enthusiastically received. Maurice did say, though, that within a few weeks someone might be found to put something together, and it was arranged that the next time one of us went down to London the equipment could be dropped off at their laboratory.

So the chances that anyone on the British side of the Atlantic would solve DNA looked small as the Christmas holidays approached. Though Francis went back to proteins, he did not enjoy simply keeping Bragg happy by working towards his Ph.D. Instead, after a few days of comparative silence, he began to talk about the alpha helix itself being arranged as part of a larger helix. I could only be sure that he would talk about DNA during the lunch hour. Fortunately, John Kendrew understood that the ban on working on DNA did not extend to thinking about it. At no time did he try to reinterest me in his work on proteins. Instead, I used the cold and dark days to learn more theoretical chemistry or to look through journals, hoping that possibly there existed a forgotten clue to DNA.

Chapter 7   TMV and RNA

I did not sit through the Christmas holidays in Cambridge. Avrion Mitchison had invited me and my sister Elizabeth to Carradale, his parents' home, in Scotland. This was real luck since over holidays Av's mother, Naomi, the famous writer, and his father, a politician, were known to fill their large home with odd mixtures of intelligent people. Moreover, Naomi was a sister of England's cleverest and most eccentric biologist, J. B. S. Haldane. Neither the feeling that our DNA work had hit a roadblock nor the uncertainty of getting paid for the year was of much concern when I joined Av and his sister Val at Euston Station. No seats were left on the overnight Glasgow train, giving us a ten-hour journey seated on luggage listening to Val comment on the dull, rude habits of the Americans who each year come to Oxford in increasing numbers.

At Glasgow we found my sister, who had flown in from Copenhagen. Dick Mitchison met our bus and drove us the thirty hilly kilometres to the tiny Scottish fishing village where he and Naomi had lived for the past twenty years. Dinner was still going on as we came out of a stone passage into a dining room dominated by sharp, confident talk. Av's scientist brother Murdoch had already come, and he enjoyed talking to people about how cells divide. More often, the subject was politics and the awkward relationship with Russia, the fault of American politicians who should be back in the law offices of mid-western towns.

By the following morning, I was aware that the best way not to feel impossibly cold was to remain in bed or, when that became impossible, to go walking, unless the rain was pouring down. In the afternoons Dick was trying to get someone to shoot pigeons, but after one attempt, when I fired the gun after the pigeons were out of sight, I spent my time lying on the living-room floor as close as possible to the fire. There was also the warming attraction of going to the library to play table tennis beneath the artist Wyndham Lewis's drawings of Naomi and her children.

More than a week passed before I slowly began to understand that a family with Labour Party connections could be bothered by the way their guests were dressed. Naomi and several of the women dressed for dinner, but I considered this odd behaviour to be a sign of approaching old age. The thought never occurred to me that my own appearance was noticed, since my hair was beginning to lose its American shortness. Odile had been very shocked when Max introduced me to her on my first day in Cambridge and afterwards had told Francis that a hairless American was coming to work in the laboratory. The best way to improve the situation was to avoid a hairdresser until I looked like other men in Cambridge. Though my sister was upset when she saw me, I knew that months, if not years, might be required to replace her shallow values with those of English intellectuals. So Carradale was the perfect environment to go one step further and acquire a beard. I did not like its reddish colour, but shaving in cold water was painful. But after a week of Val's and Murdoch's negative comments, as well as the expected unpleasantness of my sister, I came down for dinner with a clean face. When Naomi made an approving remark about my looks, I knew I had made the right decision.

In the evenings there was no way to avoid intellectual games, which gave the greatest advantage to a large vocabulary. Every time my weak contribution was read, I wanted to sink behind the chair rather than face the pitying looks of the Mitchison women. To my relief, the large number of house guests never permitted my turn to come often, and I always sat near the evening's box of chocolates, hoping no one would notice that I never passed it. Much more pleasant were the hours playing party games in the dark, twisting passages of the upstairs floors. The most determined of the games enthusiasts was Av's sister Lois, then just back from teaching for a year in Karachi.

Almost from the start of my stay, I knew that I would leave Naomi's and Dick's friends with the greatest of regret. My departure, three days after the New Year, had been fixed by an arrangement for me to speak at a London meeting of the Society for Experimental Biology. Two days before my departure there was a heavy fall of snow, giving the lifeless hills the look of Antarctic mountains. It was a perfect occasion for a long afternoon walk along the closed Campbeltown Road, with Av talking about his Ph.D experiments while I thought about the possibility that the road might still be blocked on the day I had to leave. The climate was not with me, however, because a group from the house caught the boat from Tarbert and the next morning we were in London.

On my return to Cambridge I had expected to hear from the States about whether I would receive any more money, but there was no official letter there. Since Luria had written to me in November not to worry, the absence of firm news was now disturbing. Apparently no decision had been made, and I expected the worst. However, this would only be annoying. John and Max assured me that a small English grant could be found if I was completely without money. Only in late January did the uncertainty end, with the arrival of a letter from Washington: I was sacked. The letter said that money was only available for work in the permitted place. Because I had moved from Copenhagen, they had no choice.

The second paragraph gave me the news that I had been given a completely new amount of money. This was not for the usual twelve-month period but ended after eight months, in the middle of May. My real punishment for not following the board's advice and going to Stockholm was losing a thousand dollars. By this time it was almost impossible to obtain any support which could begin before the September start of a new university year. I naturally accepted the offer. Two thousand dollars was not to be thrown away.

◆

Because I was not allowed to do anything with DNA, I decided to spend my time usefully by working on TMV, a virus that affects tobacco. An important part of TMV was nucleic acid, so it was the perfect disguise for my continuing interest in DNA. It was true that the nucleic-acid part was not DNA itself, but a second form of nucleic acid known as ribonucleic acid (RNA). However, the difference was actually an advantage, since Maurice could put forward no claim to RNA. If we solved RNA we might also provide the important clue to DNA. On the other hand, TMV was thought to have a molecular weight of 40 million and at first glance should be much more difficult to understand than the smaller molecules that John and Max had been working on for years without obtaining biologically interesting answers.

Moreover, TMV had previously been looked at with X-rays by J. D. Bernal and I. Fankucken. This was scary, since the power of Bernal's brain was famous and I could never hope to have his understanding of crystallographic theory. I was even unable to understand large sections of their great paper published just after the start of the war.

Though the theoretical basis for many of their conclusions was weak, the lesson to be learned was obvious. TMV was constructed from a large number of similar sub-units. How the sub-units were arranged they did not know. Moreover, 1939 was too early to begin thinking about the fact that the protein and

RNA parts were likely to be constructed in very different ways. By now, however, protein sub-units were easy to imagine in large numbers. Just the opposite was true of RNA. Division of the RNA part into a large number of sub-units would produce nucleotide chains too small to carry the genetic information that Francis and I believed must be contained in the viral RNA. The most believable theory for the TMV structure was a central RNA column surrounded by a large number of similar small protein sub-units.

In fact, there already existed biochemical evidence for protein building blocks. Experiments of the German Gerhard Schramm, first published in 1944, reported that TMV viruses could be broken down into free RNA and a large number of protein molecules which were similar, if not exactly alike. Almost nobody outside Germany, however, thought that Schramm's story was right. This was because of the war. It was unbelievable to most people that the Nazis would have permitted the extensive experiments that supported his claims to be routinely carried out during the last years of a war they were so badly losing. It was too easy to imagine that the work had direct Nazi support and that his experiments were incorrectly analysed. Most biochemists did not want to waste time disproving Schramm. As I read Bernal's paper, however, I suddenly became enthusiastic about Schramm; if he had misunderstood his data, by accident he had hit upon the right answer.

It was possible that a few additional X-ray pictures would tell us how the protein sub-units were arranged. This was particularly true if they were put together helically. Excitedly I borrowed Bernal's and Fankucken's paper from the Philosophical Library and brought it to the laboratory so that Francis could inspect the TMV X-ray picture. When he saw the blank areas that indicate helical patterns, he jumped into action, quickly suggesting several possible helical TMV structures. From this moment, I knew I could no longer avoid actually understanding the helical theory. Waiting until Francis had free time to help me would save me from having to master the mathematics, but only at the cost of making no progress if Francis was out of the room. Luckily, only a general understanding was needed to see why the TMV X-ray picture suggested a helix with a turn every 23 hundred-millionths of a centimetre along its length. The rules were, in fact, very simple.

This time, however, Francis did not become enthusiastic, and in the following days maintained that the evidence for a TMV helix was not strong. My spirits automatically sank, until I thought of a perfect reason why sub-units should be helically arranged. I had read a Faraday Society discussion paper on 'The Structure of Metals', which contained a clever theory by F. C. Frank on how crystals grow. Every time the calculations were properly done, the odd answer appeared that the crystals could not grow at the observed rates. Frank saw that the problem disappeared if the crystals were not as regular as suspected, but contained cracks resulting in the presence of corners into which the molecules could fit.

Several days later, on the bus to Oxford, the idea came to me that each tiny piece of TMV should be thought of as a tiny crystal growing like other crystals because it had corners. More importantly, the simplest way to produce corners was to have the sub-units helically arranged. The idea was so simple that it had to be right. Every helical staircase I saw that weekend in Oxford made me more confident that other biological structures would also have helical shapes. Francis, however, remained neutral, and in the absence of any hard facts I knew I could not change his mind.

Hugh Huxley came to my rescue by offering to teach me how to set up the X-ray camera for photographing TMV. The way to reveal a helix was to turn the TMV so that it was at several different angles to the X-ray beam. Fankucken had not done this, since before the war no one took helices seriously. So I went to Roy Markham to see if any spare TMV was available. Markham then worked in a laboratory which, unlike all the others in Cambridge, was well heated. This unusual state came from the poor health of its director, David Keilin. I always welcomed an excuse to exist temporarily at 20°C, although I was never sure when Markham would start the conversation by saying how bad I looked, implying that if I had been brought up on English beer I would not be in this poor condition. This time he was unexpectedly sympathetic and without hesitation offered some virus. The idea of Francis and me dirtying our hands with experiments amused him greatly.

My first X-ray pictures revealed, not unexpectedly, much less detail than was found in the published pictures. Over a month was required before I could get even fairly presentable pictures. They were still a long way, though, from being good enough to show a helix.

Then came the news that Linus Pauling was coming to London in May for a meeting organized by the Royal Society on the structure of proteins. One could never be sure where he would strike next. Particularly alarming was the possibility that he might ask to visit King's.

Chapter 8   Chargaff's Rules

Linus, however, was prevented from descending on London. His trip was suddenly ended through the removal of his passport. The US State Department did not want troublemakers like Pauling wandering around saying nasty things about the politics of its former investment bankers who were resisting the godless Russians. Failure to control Pauling might result in a London press conference with him arguing for a peaceful world.

Francis and I were already in London when the story reached the Royal Society. The reaction was one of almost complete disbelief. The failure to let one of the world's leading scientists attend a completely non-political meeting would have been expected from the Russians. A top Russian might easily decide to stay in the richer West. No danger existed, however, that Linus might want to run away. Only complete satisfaction with their Cal Tech existence came from him and his family.

The disaster was no surprise to several of us who had just been in Oxford for a meeting on 'The Nature of Viral Multiplication'. One of the main speakers would have been Luria. Two weeks prior to his flight to London, he was informed that he would not get a passport. As usual, the State Department would not say why.

Luria's absence meant that I got the job of describing the recent experiments of the American bacterial virus workers. There was no need to put together a speech. Several days before the meeting, Al Hershey sent me a long letter from Cold Spring Harbor summarizing the recently completed experiments by which he and Martha Chase had shown that a key feature of the infection of a bacterium by a bacterial virus was the injection of the viral DNA into the host bacterium. More importantly, very little protein entered the bacterium. Their experiment was therefore a powerful new proof that DNA is the primary genetic material.

In spite of this, almost no one in the audience of over 400 biologists seemed interested as I read long sections of Hershey's letter. Obvious exceptions were André Lwoff, Seymour Benzer, and Gunther Stent, all visiting briefly from Paris. They knew that Hershey's experiments were important and that everyone would now start to emphasize DNA. To most of the audience, however, Hershey's name meant very little. Moreover, when it came out that I was an American, my uncut hair provided no assurance that my scientific judgement was not equally eccentric. If Lwoff had not been present, the meeting would have been a total failure.

André was sympathetic to my belief that ions were highly important for nucleic-acid structure.

There was no hint at the meeting that anyone at King's had mentioned ions since the disagreement with Francis and me in early December. When I spoke to Maurice, I learned that the equipment for building the molecular models had not been touched since arriving at his laboratory. The time had not yet come to ask Rosy and Gosling to start building models. The quarrelling between Maurice and Rosy was even more bitter than before the visit to Cambridge. Now she was insisting that her data told her DNA was *not* a helix. Instead of building helical models at Maurice's command, she might twist the wire models round his neck.

When Maurice asked whether we needed the equipment back in Cambridge, we said yes, half implying that more carbon atoms were needed to make models showing how alpha helix chains turned corners. To my relief, Maurice was very open about what was not happening at King's. The fact that I was doing serious X-ray work with TMV assured him that I would not soon become interested in the DNA pattern.

◆

Maurice had no suspicion that almost immediately I would get the X-ray picture needed to prove that TMV was helical. My unexpected success came from using a powerful new X-ray tube which had just been built in the Cavendish. This permitted me to take pictures twenty times faster than before. Within a week I more than doubled the number of my X-ray photographs.

One midsummer June night, I went back to the laboratory to shut down the X-ray tube and to develop a new TMV photograph. It was leaning over at about 25 degrees, so that if I were lucky I would find the helical reflections. The moment I held the still-wet negative against the light box, I knew we had it.

The helical marks were unmistakable. Now there should be no problem in persuading Luria and Delbrück that it made sense for me to stay in Cambridge. Despite the midnight hour, I had no desire to go back to my room, and I walked happily along the riverside for over an hour.

The following morning I waited anxiously for Francis's arrival to confirm the helical conclusion. When he needed less than ten seconds to see the significant reflection, all my remaining doubts disappeared. It was now clear what we should do next. No more benefits would come quickly from TMV. Further exploration of its detailed structure needed a more professional approach than I was capable of. Moreover, it was not obvious that even the most back-breaking effort would give within several years the structure of the RNA part of the virus. The way to DNA was not through TMV.

So the moment was appropriate to think seriously about some curious regularities in DNA chemistry first observed at Columbia by the Austrian-born biochemist Erwin Chargaff. Since the war, Chargaff and his students had been carefully analysing various examples of DNA for the amounts, in relation to each other, of their purine (A and G) and pyrimidine (C and T) bases. In all their DNA preparations, the number of A molecules was very similar to the number of T molecules, while the number of G molecules was very close to the number of C molecules. Moreover, the amount of A and T, in relation to C and G, varied with the biological origin. The DNA of some life forms had an excess of A and T, while in other life forms there was an excess of G and C. No explanation for his interesting results was offered by Chargaff, though he obviously thought they were significant. When I first reported them to Francis they did not cause any reaction, and he went on thinking about other matters.

Soon afterwards, however, the suspicion that the regularities were important grew inside his head as the result of several conversations with the young theoretical chemist John Griffith. One occurred while they were drinking beer one evening after attending a scientific talk. Knowing that Griffith was interested in theoretical schemes for genes copying themselves, Francis suggested that it might be possible for a gene to copy itself exactly when the chromosome number doubles during cell division. Griffith, however, did not agree, since for some months he had preferred a scheme where gene copying was based on the alternative creation of opposite surfaces that could fit together.

This was not an original idea. It had been around for almost thirty years among theoretical geneticists. The argument said that this required the creation of a new (negative) shape where the shape was related to the original (positive) surface like a lock to a key. The negative would then use its shape to produce a new positive surface. A smaller number of geneticists could not accept this idea, but Pauling hated the idea of direct copying. Just before the war, he asked Delbrück to join him in writing a note to *Science* firmly stating their belief in a method of gene-copying which involved the production of positive and negative shapes.

Neither Francis nor Griffith was satisfied for long that evening by talking about old ideas. Both knew that the important task was to identify the attracting forces. Francis forcefully argued that hydrogen bonds were not the answer. They could not hold things in the same place since our chemist friends repeatedly told us that the hydrogen atoms in both types of base did not have fixed positions but wandered from one spot to another. Instead, Francis had the feeling that DNA copying involved particular attracting forces between the surfaces of the bases.

Luckily, this was the sort of force that Griffith might be able to calculate. If the positive-negative scheme was right, he might find attracting forces between bases with different structures. On the other hand, if direct copying existed, his calculations might reveal attraction between bases of the same type. So when the pub closed, they parted with the understanding that Griffith would see if the calculations were possible. When they met again several days later, Francis learned that there was some evidence that A and T bases should stick to each other by their flat surfaces. A similar argument could be made for attracting forces between G and C bases.

Francis immediately jumped at the answer. If his memory was correct, these were the pairs of bases that Chargaff had shown to occur in equal amounts. Excitedly he told Griffith that I had recently mentioned some odd results of Chargaff's. At the moment, though, he was not sure that the same base pairs were involved. But as soon as the data was checked, he would come round to Griffith's rooms and let him know.

At lunch I confirmed that Francis had got Chargaff's results right. But by then he was only routinely enthusiastic as he thought about Griffith's mechanical arguments. Griffith, when put under pressure, did not want to defend his exact reasoning too strongly. He had ignored too many items which might change so that he could make the calculations in a reasonable time. Moreover, though each base had two flat sides, no explanation existed for why only one side would be chosen. There was, in addition, Roy Markham's assurance that, if Chargaff said that G equalled C, he was equally certain that it did not. In Markham's eyes, Chargaff's experimental methods inevitably underestimated the true amount of C.

In spite of this, Francis was not ready to drop Griffith's scheme when, early in July, John Kendrew walked into our newly acquired office to tell us that Chargaff himself would soon be in Cambridge for an evening. John had arranged for him to have dinner at Peterhouse, and Francis and I were invited to join them later for drinks in John's room. At dinner in the College, John kept the conversation away from serious matters, only mentioning the possibility that Francis and I were going to solve the DNA structure by model-building. Chargaff, as one of the world's experts on DNA, was not at first amused by unknown scientists trying to win the race. Only when John mentioned that I was not a typical American, did he realize that he was going to listen to a madman. When he saw me, he knew he was right. Immediately he criticized my hair and accent; since I came from Chicago, I had no right to act otherwise. Telling him that I kept my hair long to avoid confusion with American Air Force personnel only proved my mental instability.

The high point in Chargaff's superiority came when he led Francis into admitting that he did not remember the chemical difference between the four bases. His later remark that he could always look them up did not persuade Chargaff that we knew where we were going or how to get there.

But however much Chargaff looked down on us, someone had to explain his results. So the next afternoon, Francis went over to Griffith's rooms in Trinity to get his ideas clear about the base-pair data. Hearing 'Come in,' he opened the door and saw Griffith with a girl. Realizing that this was not the moment for science, he slowly moved back through the door, asking Griffith to tell him again the pairs produced by his calculations. After writing them down on the back of an envelope, he left. Since I had departed that morning for continental Europe, his next stop was the Philosophical Library, where he could remove his remaining doubts about Chargaff's data. Then, with both sets of information clear in his mind, he considered returning to Griffith's rooms. But on second thoughts he realized that Griffith's interests were in another area. It was obvious that the presence of attractive young women does not inevitably lead to a scientific future.

Chapter 9   Linus Pauling

Two weeks later, Chargaff and I glanced at each other in Paris. Both of us were there for an international biochemical conference. A brief superior smile was all the recognition I got when we passed each other in the Sorbonne.* That day I was tracked down by Max Delbrück. Before I had left Copenhagen for Cambridge, he had offered me a position in the biology division of Cal Tech, to start in September 1952. This March, however, I had written to him saying that I wanted another year in Cambridge. Without any hesitation he arranged for the Cal Tech money to be transferred to the Cavendish. Delbrück's quick approval pleased me, because he had mixed feelings about the real value of Pauling-like structural studies.

With the helical TMV picture now in my pocket, I felt more confident that Delbrück would at last completely approve my liking for Cambridge. A few minutes' conversation, however, revealed no basic change in his attitude. Almost no comments came from Delbrück as I described how TMV was put together. The same unconcerned response accompanied my hurriedly delivered summary of our attempts to get DNA by model-building. Later that evening, when the geneticist Boris Ephrussi mentioned my love affair with Cambridge, Delbrück threw up his hands in disgust.

The sensation of the meeting was the unexpected appearance of Linus. Possibly because a lot had been written in the newspapers about the withdrawal of his passport, the State Department changed its mind and allowed Linus to show off the alpha helix. A lecture was hastily arranged and, despite the short notice, a large crowd arrived, hoping that they would be the first to learn of some new idea. Pauling's talk, however, was only a

*The Sorbonne: one of the oldest parts of the university in Paris.

58

humorous restatement of published ideas. It nevertheless satisfied everybody, except the few of us who knew his recent papers well. At the end, crowds of admirers surrounded him, and I did not have the courage to interrupt before he and his wife, Ava Helen, went back to their hotel.

After the conference I took the train to Royaumont for a week-long meeting on bacterial viruses. Linus Pauling was there and I briefly had him to myself after he learned that twelve months later I was coming to Cal Tech. Our conversation centred on the possibility that at Pasadena I might continue X-ray work with viruses. Almost nothing was said about DNA.

I got much further with Ava Helen. Learning that I would be in Cambridge next year, she talked about her son Peter. Already I knew that Peter had been accepted by Bragg to work towards a Ph.D with John Kendrew. This was despite the fact that his Cal Tech marks were quite low, even considering his long struggle with illness. John, however, did not want to challenge Linus's desire to place Peter with him, especially knowing that he and his beautiful blonde sister gave wonderful parties. Peter and Linda, if she visited him, would undoubtedly brighten up the Cambridge scene. When Linus signalled that they must go, I told Ava Helen that I would help her son adjust to the limited life of a Cambridge student.

A garden party at a country house brought the meeting to its end. Dressing was no easy matter for me. Just before the biochemical conference all my belongings were stolen from the train as I was sleeping. Except for a few items picked up from a shop, the clothes I still possessed had been chosen for a later visit to the Italian Alps. While I felt comfortable enough giving my talk on TMV in shorts, the French group feared that I would arrive at the garden party dressed in the same way. A borrowed jacket and tie, however, made me more or less presentable as our bus driver let us out in front of the huge country house.

I went straight to a waiter carrying drinks, and after a few minutes realized the value of a cultured upper class. Just before we had to get on the bus again, I wandered into the large sitting room dominated by paintings by Hals and Rubens. Our hostess was telling several visitors how pleased she was to have such important guests. She did regret, however, that the mad Englishman from Cambridge had decided not to come and lighten the atmosphere. For a moment I was puzzled, until I realized that Lwoff had thought it was necessary to warn the hostess about an unclothed guest who might behave eccentrically. The message of my first meeting with the upper class was clear. I would not be invited back if I acted like everyone else.

Chapter 10   News from the States

To Francis's disappointment, I showed little sign of wanting to concentrate on DNA when my summer holiday ended. I was busy thinking about sex, but not of a type that needed encouragement. There had been rumours of male and female bacteria at the Royaumont conference, but not until early September, when I attended a small meeting on genetics in Pallanza,* did I get the real facts. There, Cavalli-Sforza and Bill Hayes talked about experiments by which they and Joshua Lederberg had just proved the existence of two distinct bacterial sexes.

Bill's appearance was the surprise of the three-day gathering: before his talk nobody except Cavalli-Sforza knew he existed. As soon as he had finished his modest report, however, everyone in the audience knew that a bomb had exploded in the world of Joshua Lederberg. In 1946 Joshua, then only twenty, burst into

*Pallanza: a town in northern Italy.

the biological world by announcing that bacteria had sex with each other and showed genetic recombination. Since then he had carried out such a large number of pretty experiments that almost no one except Cavalli dared to work in the same field.

Despite Joshua's huge brain, the genetics of bacteria became messier each year. Only Joshua enjoyed the great complexity of his recent papers. Occasionally I would try to read through one, but inevitably I would get stuck and put it away for another day. No high-powered thoughts, however, were required to understand that the discovery of the two sexes might soon make the genetic analysis of bacteria quite simple. But conversations with Cavalli hinted that Joshua was not yet prepared to think simply. He liked the traditional genetic assumption that male and female cells contribute equal amounts of genetic material, even though the resulting analysis was hugely complex. In contrast, Bill's thinking started from the seemingly illogical idea that only a fraction of the male chromosomal material enters the female cell. Accepting this assumption made further thinking much simpler.

As soon as I returned to Cambridge, I went straight to the journals to which Joshua had sent his recent work. To my delight I made sense of all the previously puzzling genetic connections. A few were still impossible to explain, but the vast masses of data now falling into place made me certain that we were on the right track. Particularly pleasing was the possibility that Joshua might be so trapped in his traditional way of thinking that I could achieve the unbelievable by beating him to the correct understanding of his own experiments.

My desire to clean up Joshua's messy data had very little effect on Francis. The discovery that bacteria were divided into male and female sexes amused but did not excite him. Almost all his summer had been spent collecting dull data for his Ph.D, and now he was in a mood to think about important facts. Worrying about whether bacteria had one, two or three chromosomes would not help us find the DNA structure. If I kept reading the DNA literature, there was a chance that something might come out of lunch or teatime conversations. But if I went back to pure biology, the slight advantage we had over Linus might suddenly disappear.

At this time there was still a feeling in Francis's mind that Chargaff's rules were a real key. In fact, when I was away in Italy he had spent a week trying to prove experimentally that in water solutions there were attracting forces between A and T bases, and between G and C. But his efforts had produced nothing. In addition, he was never really comfortable talking to Griffith. Somehow, their brains did not work well together, and there would be long awkward pauses after Francis had talked through the good points of an idea. This was no reason, however, not to tell Maurice that possibly A bases were attracted to Ts, and Gs to Cs. Since he had to be in London late in October for another reason, Francis wrote a note to Maurice saying he could visit King's. The reply, inviting him to lunch, was unexpectedly cheerful, and so Francis looked forward to a serious discussion of DNA.

However, he made the mistake of politely appearing not too interested in DNA by starting to talk about proteins. Because of this, over half the lunch was wasted when Maurice changed the topic to Rosy and went on and on about her lack of cooperation. Meanwhile, Francis's mind fixed on a more amusing topic until, the meal over, he remembered he had to rush to a two-thirty meeting. Hurriedly he left the building and was out on the street before realizing he had not mentioned the agreement between Griffith's calculations and Chargaff's data. Since it would look too silly to rush back in, he went on, returning that evening to Cambridge. The following morning, after I was told about the pointlessness of the lunch, Francis tried to raise my enthusiasm for a second attempt at the structure.

Another look at DNA, however, did not make sense to me.

No new facts had come in to chase away the bad taste of last winter's disaster. Fortunately, Linus did not look like an immediate threat. Peter Pauling arrived with the news that his father was deeply involved in schemes for the coiling of alpha helices in hair protein. This was not especially good news to Francis. For almost a year he had been in and out of happy moods about how alpha helices packed together in coiled coils. The trouble was that his mathematics never worked exactly enough. When forced to, he would admit that part of his argument was uncertain. Now he faced the possibility that Linus's solution would be no better but he would still get all the recognition for the coiled coils.

Experimental work for his Ph.D was broken off so that he could work on the coiled coil mathematics with increased effort. This time the correct figures appeared, partly thanks to the help of Kreisel, who had come over to Cambridge to spend a weekend with Francis. A letter to *Nature* was quickly written and given to Bragg to send on to the editors, with a covering note asking for speedy publication. If the editors were told that a British article was of above-average interest, they would try to publish it almost immediately. With luck, Francis's coiled coils would get into print as soon as if not before Pauling's.

Because of this, there was a growing acceptance both in and outside Cambridge that Francis's brain was a genuine asset. Though a few people continued to believe he was just a laughing talking-machine, he still pursued problems to the finish line. A sign of his increasing reputation was an offer received early in the autumn to join David Harker in Brooklyn for a year. Harker was in search of talent, and the offer of six thousand dollars for one year seemed to Odile wonderfully generous. As expected, Francis had mixed feelings. There must be reasons why there were so many jokes about Brooklyn. On the other hand, he had never been to the States, and even Brooklyn would provide a base from which he could visit more pleasant regions. Also, if Bragg knew that Crick would be away for a year, he might consider a request from Max and John that Francis be reappointed for another three years after his Ph.D work was finished. It seemed best cautiously to accept the offer, and in mid-October he wrote to Harker that he would come to Brooklyn in the autumn of the following year.

As autumn passed, I remained deeply involved in the sex lives of bacteria, often going up to London to talk with Bill Hayes at his Hammersmith Hospital laboratory. My mind came back to DNA on the evenings when I managed to catch Maurice for dinner on my way home to Cambridge.

The situation with Rosy remained as difficult as ever. On his return from Brazil, the unmistakable impression was given that she considered their working relationship even more impossible than before. The question of finding Rosy a job elsewhere had been brought to his boss, Randall, but the best hope was a new position starting a year later. Sacking her immediately on the basis of her acid smile just could not be done. Moreover, her X-ray pictures were getting prettier and prettier. She gave no sign, however, of liking helices any better. In addition, she thought there was evidence that the sugar-phosphate backbone was on the outside of the molecule. There was no easy way to judge whether this point of view had any scientific basis. As long as Francis and I remained closed out from the experimental data, the best option was to maintain an open mind. So I returned to my thoughts about sex.

◆

I was by now living in Clare College. Soon after my arrival at the Cavendish, Max had slipped me into Clare as a student. The idea of working for another Ph.D was nonsense but I would only have the possibility of college rooms by using this trick. Clare was an unexpectedly happy choice. Not only was it on the River

Cam with a perfect garden but, as I learnt later, it was especially friendly to Americans.

However, during my first year at Cambridge, when I lived with the Kendrews, I saw almost nothing of college life. After being accepted as a Clare student, I went into the dining hall for several meals until I discovered that I was unlikely to meet anyone during the ten- to twelve-minute interval required to quickly eat the brown soup, stringy meat and heavy pudding provided on most evenings. Even during my second Cambridge year, when I moved into rooms in the college, I continued to avoid college food. Breakfast in the town could occur much later than if I went to the dining hall. Finding suitable evening food was trickier. Eating at the Bath Hotel was reserved for special occasions, so when Odile or Elizabeth Kendrew did not invite me to supper I ate what was served by the local Indian or Cypriot restaurants.

My stomach lasted only until early November before violent pains hit me almost every evening. Home treatment did not help and so, despite Elizabeth's assurance that nothing was wrong, I went to the ice-cold surgery of a local doctor. There I was given a large bottle of white liquid to be taken after meals. I took this for almost two weeks and then, with the bottle empty, I returned to the surgery with the fear that I had a serious stomach problem. The news that a foreigner's pains were refusing to go away did not, however, produce any sympathetic words, and I was sent to the chemist's for another bottle of white stuff.

That evening I stopped at Crick's newly bought house, hoping that gossip with Odile would make me forget my stomach. The Green Door had recently been abandoned for larger accommodation on nearby Portugal Place. Already the dull wallpaper on the lower floors was gone, and Odile was busy making curtains appropriate for a house large enough to have a bathroom. After I was given a glass of warm milk, we began discussing Peter Pauling's discovery of Nina, a Danish girl who looked after Max's children. Then we discussed the problem of how I might make a connection with the high-class guesthouse run by Camille 'Pop' Prior. The food at Pop's would offer no improvement over Clare's, but the French girls who came to Cambridge to improve their English were another matter. A seat at Pop's dinner table, however, could not be asked for directly. Instead, both Odile and Francis thought the best way to get a foot in the door would be to begin French lessons with Pop, whose husband, now dead, had lectured in French before the war. If Pop liked me, I might be invited to one of her parties and meet the current group of foreign girls. Odile promised to ring Pop and see if lessons could be arranged, and I cycled back to college with the hope that soon my stomach pains would disappear.

Back in my rooms I lit the coal fire, knowing there was no chance that the sight of my breath would disappear before I was ready for bed. With my fingers too cold to write properly, I sat next to the fire, thinking about how several DNA chains could fold together in a pretty and hopefully scientific way. Soon, however, I abandoned thinking at a molecular level and turned to the much easier job of reading biochemical papers on the relationships between DNA, RNA and the formation of proteins.

Almost all the evidence then available made me believe that DNA was the pattern on which RNA chains were made. And RNA chains were the likely candidates for the patterns for protein production. There was some uncertain data using sea life, which had been understood as DNA changing into RNA, but I preferred to trust other experiments showing that DNA molecules are very stable. So on the wall above my desk I taped up a paper sheet stating DNA → RNA → protein. The arrows did not indicate chemical changes, but instead expressed the transfer of genetic information from the order of the nucleotides in DNA molecules to the order of the units that formed protein chains.

Though I fell asleep happy with the thought that I understood the relationship between nucleic acids and the formation of protein, the shock of dressing in an ice-cold bedroom brought me back to the hard truth that a few symbols on paper did not amount to the DNA structure. Without that, the biochemists that Francis and I met in a nearby pub would continue in their belief that we would never appreciate the basic importance of complexity in biology. What was worse, even when Francis stopped thinking about coiled coils or I about bacterial genetics, we still remained stuck at the same place we were twelve months before. Lunches at the Eagle frequently went by without a mention of DNA, though usually somewhere on our after-lunch walk along the riverside genes would creep in somewhere.

On a few walks our enthusiasm would build up to the point that we played around with the models when we got back. But almost immediately Francis saw that the thinking which had given us temporary hope led nowhere. Then he would go back to the examination of his X-ray photographs, out of which his Ph.D must come. Several times I carried on alone for a half-hour or more, but without Francis's helpful chat my inability to think structurally became very obvious.

I was therefore not at all displeased that we were sharing our office with Peter Pauling, then living in Peterhouse and continuing his studies under John Kendrew. Peter's presence meant that, whenever more science was pointless, the conversation could turn to comparing girls from England, the rest of Europe and California. A pleasant face, however, was not the reason for the broad grin on Peter's face when he came into the office one afternoon in the middle of December and put his feet up on the desk. In his hand was a letter from the States that he had picked up on his return to Peterhouse for lunch.

It was from his father. In addition to the routine family gossip was the long-feared news that Linus now had a structure for

DNA. However, no details were given of what he was doing. Francis began walking up and down, thinking aloud, hoping that in a great intellectual struggle he could reconstruct what Linus might have done. Because Linus had not told us the answer, we would get equal recognition if we announced it at the same time.

Nothing useful had appeared, though, by the time we walked upstairs to tea and told Max and John about the letter. Bragg was in for a moment, but neither of us wanted to inform him that the English laboratories were again going to be beaten by the Americans. As we ate chocolate biscuits, John tried to cheer us up with the possibility that Linus might be wrong; he had never seen Maurice's or Rosy's pictures. Our hearts, however, told us otherwise.

Chapter 11   The B Form

No further news came from Pasadena before Christmas. Our spirits slowly rose; if Pauling had found a really exciting answer, the secret could not be kept for long. Even if Linus were somewhere near the correct structure, it seemed unlikely that he would get near the secret of gene copying. Also, the more we thought about DNA chemistry, the more unlikely it seemed that even Linus could work out the structure without knowing anything about the work at King's.

Maurice was told that Pauling was now working in his area when I passed through London on my way to Switzerland for a Christmas skiing holiday. I was hoping that the urgency created by Linus's assault on DNA might make him ask Francis and me for help. However, if Maurice thought that Linus had a chance to steal the prize, he did not say so. Much more important was the news that Rosy's days at King's were coming to an end. She had told Maurice that she wanted to transfer back to Bernal's laboratory at Birkbeck College.* Moreover, to Maurice's surprise and relief, she would not take the DNA problem with her. She would spend the next several months of her stay writing her work for publication. Then, with Rosy at last out of his life, he would start a thorough search for the structure.

On my return to Cambridge in mid-January, I went to find Peter to learn what was in his recent letters from home. Except for one brief reference to DNA, all the news was family gossip. The one relevant item, however, was not encouraging. A paper on DNA had been written, a copy of which would soon be sent to Peter. Again, there was not a hint of what the model looked like. While waiting for the paper to arrive, I managed to keep calm by writing down my ideas on the sex lives of bacteria. A quick visit to Cavalli in Milan, which occurred just after my skiing holiday in Zermatt, had made me believe that my ideas about how bacteria had sex were likely to be right. Since I was afraid that Lederberg might reach the same conclusions, I was anxious to publish quickly a joint article with Bill Hayes. But this was not in final form when, in the first week of February, the Pauling paper crossed the Atlantic.

Two copies, in fact, were sent to Cambridge – one to Sir Lawrence, the other to Peter. Bragg's response was to put it to one side. Not knowing that Peter would also get a copy, he hesitated to take the paper down to Max's office. There Francis would see it and set off on another chase after nothing. Under the present timetable, there were only eight months more of Francis's laugh to bear. Then for a year, if not more, with Crick far away in Brooklyn, there would be peace and quiet.

While Sir Lawrence was wondering whether to risk taking Crick's mind off his Ph.D, Francis and I were studying the copy

*Birkbeck College: a college of London University.

that Peter had brought in after lunch. Peter's face betrayed something important as he entered the door, and my stomach sank in fear at learning that all was lost. Seeing that neither Francis or I could bear to wait any longer, he quickly told us that the model was a three-chain helix with the sugar–phosphate backbone in the centre. This sounded so suspiciously like our failed effort of last year that immediately I wondered whether we might already have had the recognition and fame of a great discovery if Bragg had not held us back. Giving Francis no chance to ask for the paper, I pulled it out of Peter's outside coat pocket and began reading. By spending less than a minute with the summary and the introduction, I was soon at the figures showing the positions of the essential atoms.

At once I felt something was not right. I could not identify the mistake, however, until I looked at the illustrations for several minutes. Then I realized that the phosphate groups in Linus's model were not ionized, but that each group contained a hydrogen atom, and so had no positive or negative charge. Pauling's nucleic acid in a sense was not an acid at all. Moreover, the uncharged phosphate groups were not unimportant features. The hydrogens were part of the hydrogen bonds that held together the three twisting chains. Without the hydrogen atoms, the chains would immediately fly apart and the structure disappear.

Everything I knew about nucleic-acid chemistry indicated that hydrogen atoms were never connected to phosphate groups. No one had ever questioned that DNA was a fairly strong acid. So in a living cell, there would always be positively charged ions lying nearby to neutralize the negatively charged phosphate groups. All our thinking about whether ions held the chains together would have made no sense if there were hydrogen atoms firmly connected to the phosphates. But somehow Linus, unquestionably the world's cleverest chemist, had come to the opposite conclusion.

When Francis was equally amazed by Pauling's odd chemistry, I began to breathe more slowly. By then I knew we were still in the game. Neither of us, however, had the slightest clue to the steps that had led Linus to his great error. So we could not help worrying whether Linus's model followed from dramatic new thinking of the acid-base properties of very large molecules. The tone of the paper, however, argued against any such advance in chemical theory. No reason existed to keep secret a first-class theoretical breakthrough. If that had occurred Linus would have written two papers, the first describing his new theory, the second describing how it was used to solve the DNA structure.

The mistake was too unbelievable to keep secret for more than a few minutes. I hurried over to Roy Markham's laboratory to tell him the news and to check that Linus's chemistry was crazy. When I returned to the Cavendish, Francis was explaining to John and Max that no further time must be lost on this side of the Atlantic. Since the paper had already been sent to a journal, by mid-March at the latest it would be spread around the world. Then it would only take a few days before the error was discovered. We had about six weeks.

Though Maurice had to be warned, we did not immediately ring him. The speed of Francis's words might cause Maurice to find a reason for ending the conversation before he fully understood the situation. Since in several days I had to go up to London to see Bill Hayes, the sensible way forward was to bring the paper with me for Maurice's and Rosy's inspection.

Then, as the excitement of the last several hours had made further work that day impossible, Francis and I went out to a pub to drink to the Pauling failure. Though the chances still appeared against us, Linus had not yet won his Nobel Prize.

◆

Maurice was busy when, just before four, I walked in with the news that the Pauling model was totally wrong. So I went down the corridor to Rosy's laboratory, hoping she would be around. Since the door was already open a little, I walked in and saw her bending over a lit box. On it lay an X-ray photograph she was measuring. Surprised by my entry, she stood up and, looking straight at my face, let her eyes tell me that uninvited guests should have the politeness to knock.

I asked her whether she wanted to look at Peter's copy of his father's paper. Though I was curious how long she would take to spot the error, Rosy would not play games with me. I immediately explained where Linus had gone wrong, and I could not help pointing out the similarity between Pauling's three-chain helix and the model that Francis and I had shown her fifteen months earlier. The fact that Pauling's conclusions were no more impressive than our awkward efforts of the year before would, I thought, amuse her. The result was just the opposite. Instead, she became increasingly annoyed by my continual talk of helical structures. Coolly she pointed out that not a single piece of evidence permitted Linus, or anyone else, to imagine a helical structure for DNA. Most of my words to her were unnecessary; she knew that Pauling was wrong the moment I mentioned a helix.

Interrupting her speech, I said that the simplest form for any regular molecule made up of similar sub-units was a helix. Knowing that she might oppose this with the fact that the order of the bases was unlikely to be regular, I went on with the argument that, since DNA molecules form crystals, the nucleotide order must not affect the general structure. Rosy by then was hardly able to control her temper, and her voice rose as she told me that the stupidity of my remarks would be obvious if I would stop talking nonsense and look at her X-ray evidence.

I was more aware of her data than she realized. Several months earlier, Maurice had told me all about her 'antihelical' results.

Since Francis had assured me they led nowhere, I decided to risk a full explosion. Without further hesitation I implied that she was unable to read X-ray pictures properly. If only she would learn some theory, she would understand how her supposed antihelical features came from the minor changes in shape needed to pack regular helices into a crystalline shape.

Suddenly Rosy came from behind the laboratory table that separated us and began moving towards me. Fearing that in her anger she might strike me, I grabbed the Pauling article and hastily moved back to the open door. My escape was blocked by Maurice who, searching for me, had just then stuck his head through. While Maurice and Rosy looked at each other over my bowed head, I told Maurice that the conversation between me and Rosy was over and that I had been planning to look for him in the tea room. At the same time I was slowly moving my body from between them, leaving Maurice face to face with Rosy. Then, when Maurice failed to move away immediately, I feared that out of politeness he would ask Rosy to join us for tea. Rosy, however, removed Maurice from this uncertainty by turning round and firmly shutting the door.

Walking down the passage, I told Maurice that his unexpected appearance might have prevented Rosy from assaulting me. Slowly he assured me that this might have happened. Some months earlier she had made a similar move towards him. They had almost had a fight following an argument in his room. When he wanted to escape, Rosy had blocked the door and had moved out of his way only at the last moment. But then no third person was around.

My argument with Rosy opened up Maurice to a degree that I had not seen before. I no longer needed to imagine the emotional hell he had faced during the past two years, and he could treat me almost as a close friend. To my surprise, he revealed that with the help of his assistant Wilson he had been quietly doing some of the same X-ray work that Rosy and Gosling were doing. Because of this, there did not need to be a large time gap before Maurice's efforts were moving ahead at full speed. Then he gave me some even more important information: since the middle of the summer, Rosy had had evidence for a new form of DNA. It occurred when the DNA molecules were surrounded by a large amount of water. When I asked what the pattern was like, Maurice went into the next room to pick up a print of the new form they called the 'B' structure.

The moment I saw the picture, my mouth fell open and my heart began to beat faster. The pattern was unbelievably simpler than those obtained previously ('A' form). Moreover, the black cross of reflections which dominated the picture could come only from a helical structure. With the A form, the argument for a helix was never simple, and considerable doubt existed about the exact type of helical shape that was present. With the B form, however, simple inspection of its X-ray pictures gave several of the essential helical characteristics. Possibly, after only a few minutes' calculations, the number of chains in the molecule could be fixed. By asking Maurice what they had done using the B photo, I learned that his colleague R. D. B. Fraser had been doing some serious playing with three-chain models but had not yet found anything exciting. Though Maurice admitted that the evidence for a helix was now impossible to dismiss — the Stokes–Cochran–Crick theory clearly indicated that a helix must exist — this was not of major significance to him; he had previously thought a helix would be the answer. The real problem was the absence of any structural theory that would allow him to place the bases regularly on the inside of the helix. Of course this presumed that Rosy had been right in wanting the bases in the centre and the backbone outside. Though Maurice told me he was quite sure she was correct, I remained doubtful, because her evidence was still out of reach of Francis and me.

On our way to Soho for supper I returned to the problem of Linus, emphasizing that smiling too long over his mistake might be fatal. The position would be much safer if Pauling had just been wrong instead of looking like a fool. Soon, if not already, he would be working day and night. There was the further danger that if he asked one of his assistants to take DNA photographs, the B structure would also be discovered in Pasadena. Then, in a week at most, Linus would have the structure.

Maurice refused to get excited. As the waiter looked over his shoulder, hoping he would finally order, he made sure I understood that if we could all agree where science was going, everything would be solved and we would all have to become engineers or doctors.

Afterwards, in the cold, almost unheated train, I drew on the blank edge of a newspaper what I remembered of the B pattern. Then I tried to decide between two- and three-chain models. The reason the King's group did not like two chains was not absolutely beyond question. It depended on the amount of water in the DNA they worked with, a value they admitted might be in great error. So by the time I had cycled back to college and climbed over the back gate, I had decided to build two-chain models. Francis would have to agree. Even though he was a physicist, he knew that important biological objects come in pairs.

Chapter 12   Playing with Models

Bragg was in Max's office when I rushed in the next day to tell him what I had learned. Francis was not in yet; it was a Saturday morning and he was still at home in bed. Quickly I started to describe the details of the B form, making a rough drawing to show the evidence that DNA was a helix which repeated its pattern every 34 hundred-millionths of a centimetre along its length. Bragg soon interrupted me with a question, and I knew my argument had got across. I therefore wasted no time before mentioning the problem of Linus, giving the opinion that he was much too dangerous to be allowed a second attempt at DNA while the people on this side of the Atlantic did nothing. After saying that I was going to ask the Cavendish workshop to make models of the bases, I remained silent, waiting for Bragg to answer.

To my relief, Sir Lawrence not only made no objection, but encouraged me to get on with the job of building models. He was clearly unsympathetic to the internal fighting at King's – especially when it might allow Linus, of all people, the thrill of discovering another important molecule. Also helping us was my work on TMV. It had given Bragg the impression that I was on my own. Because of this he could fall asleep at night untroubled by the awful thought that he had given Crick permission to start work again. I then rushed down the stairs to the workshop to warn them that I was going to draw up plans for models that I wanted within a week.

Soon after I was back in our office, Francis came in to report that their last night's dinner party was a great success. Among the guests was my sister Elizabeth, who had arrived for an indefinite stay on her way back to the States. Luckily, I could install her in Camille Prior's guesthouse and arrange to take my evening meals there with Pop and her foreign girls. So Elizabeth had been saved from typical English accommodation, while I looked forward to a lessening of my stomach pains.

Also living at Pop's was Bertrand Fourcade, the most beautiful male, if not person, in Cambridge. As soon as I mentioned that we knew him, Odile expressed delight. She, like many Cambridge women, could not take her eyes off Bertrand whenever she spotted him walking in the street. Elizabeth had therefore been given the task of seeing whether Bertrand would be free to join us for a meal with the Cricks. The time finally arranged, however, was while I was in London. When I was watching Maurice carefully finish all the food on his plate, Odile had been admiring Bertrand's handsome face as he spoke of his coming summer in the south of France.

This morning, as I revealed the B pattern details, Francis saw that I did not have my usual interest in the wealthy French upper class. Especially important was my insistence that the central reflection at 3.4 hundred-millionths of a centimetre was much stronger than any other reflection. This could only mean that the 3.4 hundred-millionths of a centimetre-thick purine and pyrimidine bases were arranged on top of each other in a direction at right angles to the length of the helix. In addition, we could feel sure from both X-ray and other evidence that the distance across the helix was about 20 hundred-millionths of a centimetre.

Francis, however, would not accept my view that repeated finding of pairs in biological systems told us to build two-chain models. The way to progress, in his opinion, was to reject any argument which did not come out of the chemistry of nucleic-acid chains. Since the experimental evidence known to us could not yet show whether two- or three-chain models were more likely, he wanted to pay equal attention to both alternatives. Though I did not agree, I saw no reason to argue against him. I would, of course, start playing with two-chain models.

No serious models were built, however, for several days. Not only did we lack the bases, but we had never had the workshop put together any phosphorus atoms. Since our workshop needed three days just to turn out the simpler phosphorus atoms, I went back to Clare to work on the final version of my genetics paper. Later, when I cycled over to Pop's for dinner, I found Bertrand and my sister talking to Peter Pauling, who the week before had charmed Pop into giving him dining rights. Dinner was hardly over before Bertrand took Elizabeth off to a party, leaving Peter unsure about what to do. In the end, he came along with me to see a film.

Three days later the phosphorus atoms were ready, and I quickly put together several short sections of the sugar-phosphate backbone. Then for a day and a half I tried to find a suitable two-chain model with the backbone in the centre. All the possible models which were allowed by the B-form X-ray data, however, looked even more unsatisfactory than our three-chained models of fifteen months before. So, seeing Francis at work on his Ph.D, I took the afternoon off to play tennis with Bertrand.

During dinner at the Cricks', I was in the mood to worry about what was wrong. Though I kept insisting that we should keep the backbone in the centre, I knew none of my reasons really made sense. Finally, over coffee, I admitted that my unwillingness to place the bases inside came partly from the suspicion that it would be possible to build an enormous number of models of this type. Then we would have the impossible task of deciding whether one was right. But the real problem was the bases. If they were on the outside, we did not have to consider them. However, if they were pushed inside, the complex problem existed of how to pack together two or more chains with irregular series of bases. Here Francis had to admit that he had no ideas at all. So when I walked up out of their basement dining room into the street, I left Francis with the impression that he would have to provide at least a half-believable argument before I would seriously play about with base-centred models.

The next morning, however, as I took apart a particularly ugly backbone-centred molecule, I decide that no harm could come from spending a few days building backbone-out models. This meant temporarily ignoring the bases, but this had to happen anyway since now another week was required before the workshop could hand over the flat tin plates cut in the shapes of purines and pyrimidines.

There was no difficulty in twisting an external backbone into a shape that fitted the X-ray evidence. In fact, both Francis and I had the impression that the most satisfactory angle of turn was 30 to 40 degrees between bases. So if the backbone was on the outside, the crystallographic repeat of 34 hundred-millionths of a centimetre had to represent the distance along the helix required for a complete turn. At this stage, Francis began to get more interested, and at increasing frequencies he would look up from his calculations to glance at the model. In spite of this, neither of us had any hesitation in stopping work for the weekend. There was a party in Trinity College on Saturday night, and on Sunday Maurice was coming up to the Cricks for a social visit arranged weeks before the delivery of the Pauling paper.

Maurice, however, was not allowed to forget DNA. Almost as soon as he arrived from the station, Francis started to ask him for more details of the B pattern. But by the end of lunch Francis knew no more than I had the week before. Even the presence of Peter, saying he felt sure his father would soon leap into action, failed to change Maurice's plans. Again he emphasized that he wanted to put off more model-building until Rosy was gone, six weeks from then. Francis took the chance to ask Maurice if he would mind if we started to play about with DNA models. When Maurice's slow answer came out as no, he would not mind, my heartbeat returned to normal. Even if the answer had been yes, our model-building would have gone ahead.

◆

In the next few days Francis became increasingly disturbed by my failure to stick close to the molecular models. It did not matter that before his entrance at about ten o'clock I was usually in the laboratory. Almost every afternoon, knowing that I was on the tennis court, he would anxiously twist his head away from his work to see the nucleotide backbone unattended. Moreover, after tea I would appear for only a few minutes of minor adjustments before rushing away to have a drink with the girls at Pop's. Francis's protests did not disturb me, however, because further improvements to our latest backbone without a solution to the bases would not represent a real step forward.

I spent most evenings at the cinema, sometimes dreaming that at any moment the answer would suddenly hit me. The fact that we had produced a reasonable arrangement for the backbone was always in the back of my head. Moreover, there was no longer any fear that it would not fit the experimental data. By then it had been checked out with Rosy's exact measurements. Rosy, of course, did not directly give us her data. In fact, no one at King's realized they were in our hands. We received them because of Max's membership of a working group appointed by a government medical department to help its laboratories to work together. Since Randall wished the group to believe that he had a productive laboratory, he had instructed his people to make a comprehensive summary of their achievements. Copies of this were later sent to all the group members. The report was not secret and so Max saw no reason not to give it to Francis and me. Quickly reading through it, Francis saw with relief that following my return from King's I had correctly reported to him the essential features of the B pattern. So only minor changes were necessary in our background arrangement.

Generally, it was late in the evening after I got back to my rooms when I tried to puzzle out the mystery of the bases. These were described in J. N. Davidson's little book *The Biochemistry of Nucleic Acids*. I kept a copy of this in Clare so I could be sure that I had the correct structures when I drew tiny pictures of the bases on sheets of Cavendish notepaper. My aim was somehow to arrange the centrally positioned bases in such a way that the backbones on the outside were completely regular – giving the sugar-phosphate group of each nucleotide the same arrangement in space. But each time I tried to find a solution, I hit the problem that the four bases each had a quite different shape. Moreover, there were many reasons to believe that the orders of the bases of any nucleotide chain were very irregular. Because of this, unless some very special trick existed, just twisting two nucleotide chains around one another should result in a mess. In some places the bigger bases must touch each other, while in other regions, where the smaller bases would lie opposite each other, there must either be a gap or else the backbone regions must bend in.

There was also the worrying problem of how the twisted chains might be held together by hydrogen bonds between the bases. Though for over a year Francis and I had dismissed the possibility that bases formed regular hydrogen bonds, it was now obvious to me that we had done so incorrectly. The observation that one or more hydrogen atoms on each of the bases could move from one position to another had initially led us to the conclusion that all the possible forms of any particular base occurred in equal frequencies. But a recent rereading of J. M. Gulland's and D. O. Jordan's papers on the reaction of DNA with acids and bases made me finally appreciate the strength of their conclusion that a large fraction, if not all, of the bases formed hydrogen bonds to other bases. Even more important, these hydrogen bonds were present at very low amounts of DNA, strongly hinting that the bonds linked together the bases in the same molecule. There was, in addition, the X-ray crystallographic result that each pure base that had been examined formed as many irregular hydrogen bonds as was physically possible. So it was possible that the heart of the matter was a rule governing hydrogen bonds between bases.

My drawing of the bases on paper got nowhere and I fell asleep hoping that a party the next afternoon at Downing College would be full of pretty girls. But my heart sank as soon as

I arrived and saw a group of healthy sportswomen and several pale daughters of the upper class. Bertrand also quickly realized he was out of place, and as we stood for a polite period before leaving, I explained how I was racing Peter's father for the Nobel Prize.

Not until the middle of the next week, however, did a useful idea appear. It came while I was drawing the joined rings of A bases on paper. Suddenly, I realized the enormous possibilities presented by a DNA structure in which the A bases formed hydrogen bonds similar to those in pure A crystals. If DNA was like this, each A base would form two hydrogen bonds to another A related to it by an 18-degree turn. Most importantly, two hydrogen bonds could also hold together pairs of G, C or T bases. So I started wondering whether each DNA molecule consisted of two chains with bases in the same order held together by hydrogen bonds between pairs of the same type of bases. There was the complication that such a structure could not have a regular backbone, since the purines (A and G) and the pyrimidines (T and C) have different shapes. The resulting backbone would have to show some minor in-and-out bends depending on whether pairs of purines or pyrimidines were in the centre.

Despite the messy backbone, my heart began to race. If this was DNA, I would create a sensation by announcing its discovery. The existence of two twisted chains with bases in the same order could not be a matter of chance. Instead it would strongly suggest that one chain in each molecule had at some earlier stage served as the pattern for the production of other chains. Under this scheme, each copy starts with the separation of its two matching chains. The two new daughter chains are made on the two parental patterns, forming two DNA molecules exactly the same as the original molecule. So the essential trick of gene copying could come from the requirement that each base in the newly produced chain always bonds through hydrogen to a

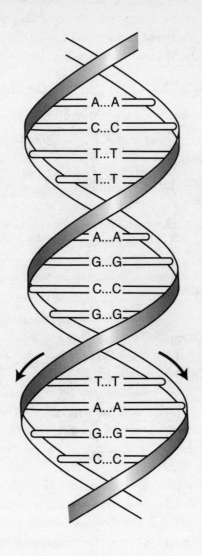

A view of a DNA molecule built up from like-with-like base pairs;
pairs where each base connects with another of the same type.

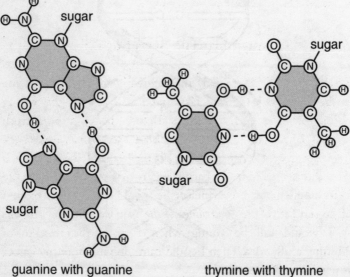

adenine with adenine

cytosine with cytosine

guanine with guanine

thymine with thymine

The four base pairs used to construct a like-with-like structure.
(Hydrogen bonds are dotted.)

base of the same type. That night, however, I could not see why the common form of G base would not connect in this way to an A. Similarly, several other pairing mistakes should also occur. But there was no reason to be disturbed by this; there might be substances present that always caused bases to bond with others of the same type.

As the clock went past midnight, I was becoming more and more pleased. There had been too many days when Francis and I worried that the DNA structure might actually be very dull, suggesting nothing about the way it copied itself or its role in controlling biochemistry. But now, to my delight and amazement, the answer was extremely interesting. For over two hours I happily lay awake with a pair of A bases turning in front of my closed eyes. Only for brief moments did the fear shoot through me that such a good idea could be wrong.

Chapter 13   The Secret of Life

My scheme was destroyed by the following midday. Against me was the awkward chemical fact that I had chosen the wrong physical forms of G and T bases. Before this disturbing truth came out, I had eaten a hurried breakfast, then briefly gone back into Clare to reply to a letter from Max Delbrück which reported that my article on bacterial genetics looked faulty to the Cal Tech geneticists. Nevertheless, he would agree to my request that he send it to the *Proceedings of the National Academy*. In this way I would still be young when I made the mistake of publishing a silly idea. Then I could calm down before my career was permanently destroyed.

At first this message worried me – as it was meant to. But now, with my spirits being lifted by the possibility that I had the self-copying structure, I said again that I knew what happened when bacteria had sex. Moreover, I could not help adding a sentence saying I had just worked out a beautiful DNA structure which was completely different from Pauling's. For a few seconds I considered giving some details, but since I was in a rush I decided not to, quickly dropped the letter in the box, and raced off to the laboratory.

The letter was not in the post for more than an hour before I knew that my claim was nonsense. No sooner had I got to the office and begun explaining my scheme than the American crystallographer Jerry Donohue protested that the idea would not work. The physical forms I had copied out of Davidson's book were, in Jerry's opinion, incorrect. My immediate response that several other texts also pictured G and T bases in these forms failed to impress Jerry. Happily he revealed that for years organic chemists had been preferring particular physical forms to their alternatives on the basis of very little evidence. In fact, organic-chemistry textbooks were full of pictures of extremely improbable physical forms. The G picture I was pushing towards his face was almost certainly false. All his chemical experience told him that it would occur in the other form. He was just as sure that the T base was also given the wrong form. Again, he strongly favoured the alternative. So I was firmly urged not to waste more time with my crazy scheme.

Though my immediate reaction was to hope that Jerry was wrong, I did not dismiss his criticism. Jerry knew more about hydrogen bonds than anyone else in the world except Linus himself. Since for many years he had worked at Cal Tech on the crystal structures of small organic molecules, I could not deceive myself that he did not understand our problem. During the six months that he had occupied a desk in our office, I had never heard him talking about subjects about which he knew nothing.

Thoroughly worried, I went back to my desk hoping that I could think of a way to save the like-with-like idea. But it was obvious that the new structures were its death blow. Shifting the hydrogen atoms to their alternative positions made the size differences between the purines and pyrimidines even more important than they would be if only my chosen forms existed. I could only imagine the nucleotide backbone bending enough to cope with the irregular order of the bases by proposing the most extreme argument. Even this possibility disappeared when Francis came in. He immediately realized that a like-with-like structure would mean a turning angle between neighbouring bases of only 18 degrees, a value Francis believed to be impossible after his recent playing with the models. Also, Francis did not like the fact that the structure gave no explanation for the Chargaff rules (A-type equals T, G-type equals C). I, however, was still not so enthusiastic about Chargaff's data.

After lunch I was not anxious to return to work; I was afraid that while trying to fit the alternative forms of G and T bases into some new scheme I would run into a stone wall and have to face the fact that no regular hydrogen-bonding scheme would fit the X-ray evidence. As long as I remained outside looking at the flowers, I could continue to hope that a pretty base arrangement would appear. Fortunately, when we walked upstairs, I found that I had an excuse to put off the important model-building step for at least several more hours. The metal purine and pyrimidine models needed for systematically checking all the imaginable hydrogen-bonding possibilities had not been finished on time. At least two more days were needed before they would be in our hands. This was much too long for me to remain idle, so I spent the rest of the afternoon cutting the shapes of the bases out of stiff cardboard. But by the time they were ready, I realized that the answer must be put off till the next day. After dinner I was joining Pop's group at the theatre.

When I got to our still empty office the following morning, I quickly cleared away the papers from my desk top so that I could have a large flat surface on which to form pairs of bases held

ENOL   KETO

thymine

guanine

The contrasting physical forms of G and T bases which might occur in DNA. The hydrogen atoms that can undergo changes in position are shaded.

together by hydrogen bonds. Though I initially went back to my like-with-like preferences, I soon realized that they led nowhere. When Jerry came in I looked up, saw that it was not Francis, and began shifting the bases in and out of various other pairing possibilities. Suddenly I became aware that an A-T pair held together by two hydrogen bonds was exactly the same shape as a G-C pair held together by at least two hydrogen bonds. All the hydrogen bonds seemed to form naturally; no changes were necessary to make the two types of base pairs the same shape. Quickly I called Jerry over to ask him whether this time he had any objection to my new base pairs.

When he said no, my spirits leapt; I suspected that we now had the answer to the puzzle of why the number of purines exactly equalled the number of pyrimidines. Two irregular series of bases could be regularly arranged in the centre of a helix if a purine always hydrogen-bonded to a pyrimidine. Furthermore, the hydrogen-bonding requirement meant that A would always pair with T, while G would always pair with C. Chargaff's rules then suddenly became a consequence of a double-helical structure for DNA. Even more exciting, this type of double helix suggested a copying scheme much more satisfactory than my briefly considered like-with-like pairing. Always pairing A with T and G with C meant that when the order of the bases of one chain was in place, their order in its partner was automatically determined.

On his arrival Francis did not get more than halfway through the door before I said that the answer to everything was in our hands. Though as a matter of principle he remained doubtful for a few moments, the similarly shaped A-T and G-C pairs had their expected effect. He quickly pushed the bases together in a number of other ways but did not reveal any other way to satisfy Chargaff's rules.

The question then became whether the A-T and G-C base pairs would easily fit the backbone structure we had built during

The A-T and G-C base pairs used to construct the double helix. (Hydrogen bonds are dotted.) The formation of a third hydrogen bond between G and C was considered but rejected because a crystallographic study of G itself hinted that it would be very weak. Now this idea is known to be wrong. Three strong hydrogen bonds can be drawn between the G and C.

the previous two weeks. At first glance this looked likely, since I had left free in the centre a large vacant area for the bases. However, we both knew that we would not be sure until a complete model was built in which all the contacts were satisfactory. There was also the obvious fact that the consequences of its existence were much too important for it to be released unchecked. So I felt slightly uncomfortable when Francis rushed into the pub to tell everyone within hearing distance that we had found the secret of life.

Chapter 14   Spreading the News

Francis's involvement in DNA quickly became full time. The first afternoon following the discovery that A–T and G–C base pairs had similar shapes, he went back to work on his Ph.D, but his effort was ineffective. He would constantly jump up from his chair, look worriedly at the cardboard models, play around with other combinations, and then, after a brief period of uncertainty, look satisfied and tell me how important our work was. It seemed almost unbelievable that the DNA structure was solved, that the answer was immensely exciting, and that our names would be connected with the double helix as Pauling's was with the alpha helix.

When the pubs opened at six, I went for a drink with Francis to talk about what must be done in the next few days. Francis wanted no time lost in seeing whether a satisfactory structural model could be built. Though I was equally anxious about this, I thought more about Linus and the possibility that he might find the base pairs before we told him the answer.

That night, however, we could not confirm the double helix. Until the metal bases were ready, any model building would be too inexact to be convincing. I went back to Pop's to tell

Elizabeth and Bertrand that Francis and I had probably beaten Pauling to the answer and that it would revolutionize biology. Both were genuinely pleased, Elizabeth with sisterly pride, Bertrand with the idea that he could report back to his rich friends that he knew somebody who would win a Nobel Prize. Peter's reaction was equally enthusiastic and he gave no sign that he minded the possibility of his father's first scientific defeat.

The following morning I felt marvellously alive when I awoke. On my way to breakfast I slowly walked towards the Clare Bridge, staring up at the high points of King's College that stood out sharply against the spring sky. I briefly stopped and looked over at the perfect features of the recently cleaned Gibbs Building, thinking that much of our success was due to the long uneventful periods when we walked among the colleges or quietly read the new books that came into Heffer's Bookstore. After happily reading *The Times*, I wandered into the laboratory to see Francis, unusually early, turning the cardboard base pairs back and forward over an imaginary line. Both sets of base pairs seemed to fit neatly into the backbone arrangement. As the morning moved on, Max and then John came by to see if we still thought we had solved it. Each got a quick lecture from Francis, during the second of which I wandered down to see if the workshop could be speeded up to produce the purines and pyrimidines later that afternoon.

Only a little encouragement was needed to get the work finished in the next couple of hours. The brightly shining metal plates were then immediately used to make a model in which for the first time all the different parts of DNA were in place. In about an hour I had arranged the atoms in positions which satisfied both the X-ray data and the laws of chemistry. The resulting helix was right-handed with the two chains running in opposite directions. Only one person can easily play with a model, so Francis did not try to check my work until I had backed away and said that I thought everything fitted. While two of the atoms were slightly closer to each other than we would have liked, the distance was not out of line with several published values, and I was not worried. Another fifteen minutes playing around by Francis failed to find anything wrong, though for brief intervals my stomach felt uncomfortable when I saw him frowning. In each case he became satisfied and moved on to check that another interatomic contact was reasonable. Everything therefore looked very good when we went back to have supper with Odile.

At dinner we spoke about how to let the big news out. Maurice, especially, must soon be told. But remembering the disaster of sixteen months before, keeping the secret from King's made sense until exact positions had been obtained for all the atoms. It was too easy to make up what seemed like a successful series of atomic contacts so that, while each looked almost acceptable, the whole collection was energetically impossible. So the next several days must be spent working out the positions of all atoms in a single nucleotide in relation to each other. Because the helix was made up of similar nucleotides, the positions of the atoms in one would automatically give us the other positions.

The next morning I again found that Francis had beaten me to the laboratory. He was already at work tightening the model on its support stands so he could work out the atomic positions. While he moved the atoms back and forward, I sat on top of my desk thinking about what to put in the letters I could soon write, saying that we had found something interesting. Occasionally Francis would look disgusted when my daydreams prevented me from observing that he needed help to stop the model collapsing while he rearranged the supporting stands.

Bragg had his first look late that afternoon. For several days he had been ill, and he was in bed when he heard that Crick and I had thought of an original DNA structure which might be important to biology. During his first free moment back in the Cavendish, he slipped away from his office for a direct view. Immediately he noticed the equal but opposite relationship between the two chains and saw how a pairing of A with T and G with C was a logical consequence of the repeating shape of the sugar-phosphate backbone. As he was not aware of Chargaff's rules, I told him about the experimental evidence on the quantities of the various bases in relation to each other, noticing that he was becoming increasingly excited by its possible implications for gene copying. When the question of X-ray evidence came up, he saw why we had not yet called the King's group. He was bothered, however, that we had not yet asked Todd's opinion. Telling Bragg that we had got the organic chemistry right did not completely satisfy him. The chance that we were using the wrong chemistry was small, but since Crick talked so fast, Bragg could never be sure that he would ever slow down for long enough to get the right facts. So it was arranged that as soon as we had a set of atomic measurements, we would ask Todd to come over.

The finishing touches to the positions were made the following evening. Lacking the exact X-ray evidence, we were not confident that the arrangement chosen was absolutely correct. But this did not bother us; we only wished to show that at least one definite, two-chain helix with paired bases was chemically possible. Until this was clear, the objection could be raised that, although our idea was artistically pleasing, the shape of the sugar-phosphate backbone might not permit its existence. Happily, we now knew that this was not true, and so we had lunch, telling each other that such a pretty structure just had to exist.

With the tension now at an end, I went to play tennis with Bertrand, telling Francis that later in the afternoon I would write to Luria and Delbrück about the double helix. It was also

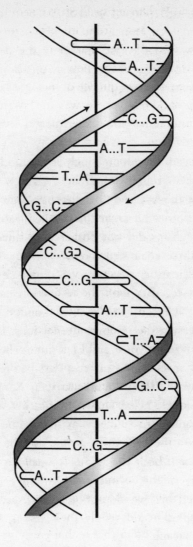

An illustration of the double helix. The two sugar-phosphate backbones twist about on the outside with the flat hydrogen-bonded base pairs forming the centre. Seen this way, the structure looks like a winding staircase with the base pairs forming the steps.

arranged that John Kendrew would call Maurice to say he should come out to see what Francis and I had just produced. Neither Francis nor I wanted the task. Earlier in the day the post had brought a note from Maurice to Francis, mentioning that he was now going to start working full time on DNA and intended to emphasize model-building.

◆

Maurice only needed a minute's look at the model to like it. He had previously been told by John that it was a two-chain version, held together by the A–T and G–C base pairs, and so immediately on entering our office he studied its detailed features. That it had two, not three, chains did not bother him, since he knew the evidence for a three-chain structure never seemed very clear.

The next scientific step was to compare seriously the experimental X-ray data with the diffraction pattern predicted by our model. Maurice went back to London, saying that he would soon measure the important reflections. There was not a hint of bitterness in his voice, and I felt quite relieved.

He was back in London only two days before he rang up to say that both he and Rosy found that their X-ray data strongly supported the double helix. They were quickly writing up their results and wanted to publish at the same time as our announcement of the base pairs. *Nature* was the place for rapid publication, since if both Bragg and Randall strongly supported the papers, they might be published within a month of their receipt. However, there would not be just one paper from King's. Rosy and Gosling would report their results separately from Maurice and his team.

Rosy's immediate acceptance of our model at first amazed me. I had feared that her sharp, determined mind, caught in her self-made antihelical trap, might dig up irrelevant results that would cause uncertainty about the correctness of the double helix.

However, like everyone else, she saw the appeal of the base pairs and accepted the fact that the structure was too pretty not to be true. Moreover, even before she learned of our proposal, the X-ray evidence had been forcing her more than she liked to admit towards a helical structure. The positioning of the backbone on the outside of the molecule was demanded by her evidence and, since it was necessary to hydrogen-bond the bases together, the uniqueness of the A–T and G–C pairs was a fact she saw no reason to argue about.

At the same time her fierce annoyance with Francis and me collapsed. Initially we were hesitant to discuss the double helix with her, fearing the anger of our previous meetings. But Francis noticed her changed attitude when he was in London to talk with Maurice about details of the X-ray pictures. Thinking that Rosy wanted to avoid him, he spoke largely to Maurice, until he slowly noticed that Rosy wanted his crystallographic advice and was prepared to exchange open opposition for conversation between equals. With obvious pleasure Rosy showed Francis her data, and for the first time he was able to see how reliable her statement was that the sugar-phosphate backbone was on the outside of the molecule.

Obviously affecting this change in Rosy's attitude was her appreciation that our past talk about model-building represented a serious approach to science, not a lazy alternative. It also became apparent to us that Rosy's difficulties with Maurice and Randall were connected with her understandable need for being equal to the people she worked with.

Two letters from Pasadena that week brought the news that Pauling was still a long way from the answer. The first came from Delbrück, saying that Linus had just given a talk during which he described an altered version of his DNA structure. Unusually, the paper he had sent to Cambridge had been published before his colleague, R. B. Corey, could accurately measure the interatomic distances. When this was finally done, they found several unacceptable contacts that could not be overcome by minor adjustments. Pauling hoped, however, to save the situation by an alteration suggested by his colleague Vermeer Schomaker. In the new form the phosphate atoms were twisted 45 degrees, which allowed a different group of oxygen atoms to form a hydrogen bond. After Linus's talk, Delbrück told Schomaker he was not sure that Linus was right, because he had just received a note saying that I had a new idea for the DNA structure.

Delbrück's comments were passed on immediately to Pauling, who quickly wrote a letter to me. The first part betrayed nervousness – and it contained an invitation to a meeting on proteins to which he had decided to add a section on nucleic acids. Then he openly asked for the details of the beautiful new structure I had written to Delbrück about. Reading his letter, I took a deep breath, because I realized that Delbrück had not known about the new double helix at the time of Linus's talk. Instead, he was referring to the like-with-like idea. Fortunately, by the time the letter reached Cal Tech, we had the base pairs properly arranged. If this had not happened, I would have been in the awful position of having to inform Delbrück and Pauling that I had foolishly written about an idea which was only twelve hours old and lived only twenty-four hours before it was dead.

Todd made his official visit late in the week, coming over from the chemical laboratory with several younger colleagues. Francis's quick description of the structure and its implications lost none of its energy, though it had been given several times each day for the past week. The level of his excitement was rising every day, and generally, whenever Jerry or I heard the voice of Francis bringing in some new faces, we left our office until they were let out and some sort of work could start again. Todd was a different matter; I wanted to hear him tell Bragg that we had correctly followed his advance on the chemistry of the sugar-phosphate backbone. Todd also agreed with the forms we had used for G-type and T-type bases, saying that his organic-chemist friends had drawn the alternatives for no particular scientific reason. Then he went off, after congratulating Francis and me on our excellent chemical work.

Soon I left Cambridge to spend a week in Paris. A trip to Paris to be with Boris and Harriet Ephrussi had been arranged some weeks earlier. Since the main part of our work seemed finished, I saw no reason to postpone a visit which now had the added attraction of letting me be the first to tell Ephrussi's and Lwoff's laboratories about the double helix. Francis, however, was not happy, telling me that a week was too long to abandon work of such extreme significance. A call for seriousness, however, had no effect on me – especially when John had just shown Francis and me a letter from Chargaff in which he asked for information on what his scientific fools were doing.

Chapter 15　'We wish to suggest a structure . . .'

Pauling first heard about the double helix from Delbrück. At the bottom of the letter that broke the news of the chains with different types of bases in pairs, I had asked him not to tell Linus. I was still slightly afraid that something would go wrong and did not want Pauling to think about hydrogen-bonded base pairs until we had a few more days to think about our position. My request, however, was ignored. Delbrück wanted to tell everyone in his laboratory and knew that within hours the gossip would travel from his colleagues to their friends working under Linus. Also, Pauling had made him promise to let him know as soon as he heard from me. Then there was the even more important fact that Delbrück hated any form of secrecy in scientific matters and did not want to keep Pauling waiting any longer.

Pauling's reaction was one of genuine excitement, as was Delbrück's. In almost any other situation Pauling would have fought for the good points of his idea. The tremendous advantages of a base-paired DNA molecule made him accept that he had lost the race. He did want, however, to see the evidence from King's before he considered the matter final. This he hoped would be possible three weeks later, when he would come to Brussels for a meeting in the second week of April.

We discovered that Pauling knew when we received a letter from Delbrück just after I returned from Paris on 18 March. By then we did not mind, because the evidence for the base pairs was steadily growing.

While I was away, Francis had started to look at the structure of the DNA molecule in the A form. Previous work in Maurice's laboratory had shown that crystalline A-form DNA strings increase in length when they take up water and go over into the B form. Francis guessed that the shorter A form was achieved by leaning the base pairs over. So he started building a model with leaning bases. Though this turned out to be more difficult to fit together than the more open B structure, a satisfactory A model was waiting for me on my return.

In the next week, early versions of our *Nature* paper were handed out and two were sent to London for comments from Maurice and Rosy. They had no real objections. Both Rosy's and Maurice's papers covered approximately the same ground and in each case saw their results in terms of base pairs. For a while, Francis wanted to expand our note to write at length about the biological implications. But finally he realized that a short remark would be better and wrote a sentence saying that the pairing we had described immediately suggested a possible copying system for the genetic material.

Sir Lawrence was shown the paper in its nearly final form. After suggesting a minor alteration, he enthusiastically expressed his willingness to post it to *Nature* with a strong accompanying letter. The solution to the structure was bringing genuine happiness to Bragg. It was obviously important that the results came out of the Cavendish and not from Pasadena. The unexpectedly marvellous nature of the answer was even more important, and so was the fact that the X-ray method he had developed forty years before was at the heart of a new understanding of the nature of life itself.

The final version was ready to be typed on the last weekend of March. Our Cavendish typist was not around, and the brief job was given to my sister. There was no problem persuading her to spend a Saturday afternoon in this way, because we told her that she was taking part in perhaps the most famous event in biology since Darwin's book. Francis and I stood over her as she typed the 900-word article that began, 'We wish to suggest a structure for the salt of deoxyribose nucleic acid (DNA).' On Tuesday, the article was sent up to Bragg's office and on Wednesday, 2 April, it went off to the editors of *Nature*.

Linus arrived in Cambridge on Friday night. On his way to Brussels for his meeting he came to see Peter and to look at the model. Unthinkingly Peter arranged for him to stay at Pop's. Soon we found that he would have preferred a hotel. The presence of foreign girls at breakfast did not compensate for the lack of hot water in his room. On Saturday morning Peter brought him into the office, where, after greeting Jerry with Cal Tech news, he started examining the model. Though he still wanted to see the quantitative measurements of the King's laboratory, we supported our argument by showing him a copy of Rosy's original photograph. After this, he gracefully gave his opinion that we had the answer.

Elizabeth and I flew the following afternoon to Paris, where Peter would join us the next day. Ten days later, she was sailing to the States on her way to Japan to marry an American she had known in college. These were our last days together, at least in the light-hearted spirit that marked our escape from the Middle West and the American culture it was so easy to have mixed feelings about. On Monday morning we went over to the Faubourg St Honoré for our last look at its elegance. There, looking in at a shop full of fashionable umbrellas, I realized that one should be her wedding present and we quickly bought it. Afterwards she met a friend for tea while I walked back across the River Seine to our hotel. Later that night, with Peter, we would celebrate my birthday. But now I was alone, looking at the long-haired girls near St Germain des Prés and knowing they were not for me. I was twenty-five and too old to be unusual.

ACTIVITIES

Chapters 1–5

Before you read

1 These words are all used in this book. Check their meanings in a scientific dictionary. Then use them to complete the text below.

   chromosomes   deoxyribonucleic   genes   helix   molecule
   nucleic   nucleotides   proteins   structure   X-ray diffraction

   ..... acids are made up of long chains of ..... . The most important of these is ..... acid, or DNA. Each ..... of DNA consists of two chains twisted into a double ..... . Its ..... was first investigated using a photographic method known as .... are formed from lengths of DNA. Thread-like structures made up of DNA and ..... are known as ....

2 Match these words to the definitions below. Use a good dictionary if necessary.

   bacteria   bio-   board   bond   crystal   Ph.D   purine
   pyrimidine

   a a force of attraction
   b relating to life, or living things
   c an advanced university degree
   d a group of people who make decisions
   e single living cells which might cause disease
   f a type of nucleotide base, shaped like two linked circles with branches
   g a type of nucleotide base, shaped like a circle with branches
   h a solid mass of atoms or molecules with a regular form and flat surfaces

3 Find a connection between each of these words and a pair of words below.

   alpha   carbon   hydrogen   ion   neutral   phosphate   virus

   a first, Greek   e gas, burns
   b illness, tiny   f chemical, complex
   c coal, diamonds   g atom, charged
   d not positive, not negative

4 James Watson and Francis Crick met in Cambridge in 1951. They were both interested in DNA, but hesitated to start work on it. Why, do you think? Which of these reasons seem more likely?

   a They did not have the necessary technology.

   b Somebody else was working on it.

   c They were not qualified.

   d US scientists had already solved most of the problem.

   e They felt that proteins might be more interesting.

After you read

5 James Watson says he managed to avoid learning any chemistry until after he had completed his Ph.D. This is not perhaps the most obvious preparation for his later work. Discuss the idea that answers sometimes come from taking an indirect approach to a problem.

6 Read about the argument between Francis Crick and Sir Lawrence Bragg in the first three paragraphs of Chapter 4 (pages 25–26). Crick is sure that Bragg stole his idea. Bragg is equally sure that he did not. With another student, act out the argument from Crick's arrival at Bragg's office. Try to use what you know of the character and personalities of the two men.

Chapters 6–10

Before you read

7 Watson and Crick are going to build a model of DNA. What do you think the result will be?

   a It will be reasonably accurate but will need months of further work.

   b It will be wrong, but they will be encouraged to try again.

   c It will be wrong, and they will be told to stop work on DNA.

8 Match these words to the definitions below. Use a good dictionary if necessary.

   coil   phosphorus   ribonucleic acid   TMV

   a a virus which attacks the tobacco plant

   b the full form of RNA

   c shaped like a metal spring

d a poisonous chemical which catches fire in air and gives light in the dark

After you read

9 Decide whether these statements are true or false. Correct the false ones.

    a The DNA model that Watson and Crick showed to the King's College group was wrong partly because Franklin had miscalculated the water content of DNA.

    b After he was stopped from working on DNA, Watson decided to work on TMV because it contained a nucleic acid.

    c Chargaff discovered that the amounts of A and T bases in DNA were similar.

    d Most of Linus's lecture audience in Paris were happy with his lecture because they were very familiar with his recent work.

    e Watson believed that DNA changed chemically into RNA and then into protein.

10 Watson and Crick believe they can solve DNA by building a model that fits the theory. Franklin and Wilkins think the answer will come through experimental work. In general, which of these scientific methods do you think is the most effective? Discuss your ideas with another student.

Chapters 11–15

Before you read

11 In February 1953, Watson and Crick see a copy of the letter in which Linus Pauling describes his structure for DNA. Read the sentences below and decide which one you think is most likely to be true.

    a Pauling describes the correct structure, but it is so similar to Watson and Crick's earlier model that they get the recognition.

    b Pauling, the world's greatest chemist, makes a basic mistake in the chemistry.

    c Linus's structure is wrong in one detail. Watson and Crick see the problem, change it and produce the correct structure.

After you read

12 If Watson and Crick had not begun to work on DNA, the answer would probably have been found, within a fairly short time, either by the King's College group or by Linus Pauling. Do you think they were right to do what they did? Discuss your ideas with another student.

13 Many people, including, later, Watson himself, feel he was unfair to Rosalind Franklin in *The Double Helix*. In fact, one of her friends later wrote a book (*Rosalind Franklin and DNA* by Anne Sayre, W. W. Norton, New York 1975) to correct some of the things that Watson said about her. You might like to find a copy of this and read it. Alternatively, try searching under her name on the Internet and find out more about this scientist's life.

Writing

14 James Watson arrived in Cambridge in autumn 1951. He found a town with beautiful buildings, talented people, damp and unheated houses, bad food and cold weather. Write a letter from him to his sister Elizabeth describing how he feels about living and working there.

15 The important models for the helix were, 1) three chains with the backbones inside, 2) two chains with the backbones outside, using like-with-like base pairs, 3) the same using mixed base pairs. Write a description of the thinking behind each model, and explain why the first two were rejected.

16 Read the first paragraph of Chapter 15, beginning, 'Pauling first heard about the double helix from Delbrück.' Imagine you are Delbrück. Write a letter back to James Watson explaining why you told Pauling despite his wishes.

17 Read the three paragraphs about Rosalind Franklin beginning with, 'Rosy's immediate acceptance of our model at first amazed me,' on page 96. Now look back at the information given about her in the Introduction. Do you feel that Watson gives Franklin enough recognition for her contribution to the discovery of the double helix?

18 'Francis's quick description of the structure and its implications lost none of its energy, though it had been given several times each day for the past week.' (page 98) Imagine you are Francis Crick, explaining the double helix to a group of visitors. Write what you will say.

19 In the 1950s scientists were still highly respected, and names like Crick and Watson became well known. In Britain and in many other countries this has changed in the years since then, and it is now much more difficult to persuade young people to consider science as a career. What are the reasons for the difference in the way many people see scientists?

BESTSELLING
PENGUIN READERS

AT LEVEL 6

Brave New World

The Chamber

Cry, the Beloved Country

Great Expectations

Kolymsky Heights

Memoirs of a Geisha

Misery

Oliver Twist

Presumed Innocent

The Remains of the Day

Saving Private Ryan

Snow Falling on Cedars